The Harvest Principle
and the
Generation Concept
in

The Proclamation of
The Acceptable Year
of the LORD

Camp Meeting 2004
By Dr. Elliot O. Douglin

The Harvest Principle
and the Generation Concept in
The Proclamation of
The Acceptable Year
of the LORD

Camp Meeting 2004
By Dr. Elliot O. Douglin

Truth for the Final Generation
P.O. Box 725
Bridgetown, Barbados, W.I.
Tel/Fax (246) 421-7297
email: truth@sunbeach.net

Truth for the Final Generation
P.O. Box 216 Caldwell, Idaho 83606
email: info@TruthInJesus.org

Visit us on the web at **http://www.TruthInJesus.org**

International Standard Book Number: 0-9741841-3-6

Printed in the United States of America   2 3 4 5 6 7 8 9 10
First Printing: July 2004

Cover design and book design by Sawtooth Graphics, Caldwell, ID, USA

Preface

Welcome to our 2004 Camp-meeting! Our main theme for this camp is one of solemn urgency:

The Proclamation Of The Acceptable Year Of The Lord.

In these lectures we are examining the reasons for the long delay of the Second Advent and what must be our responsibilities if we are to hasten the day of the LORD and finish the work early in this new generation.

The God-sent light has been building up especially since the year 2000. Please make sure that you obtain and study each of the following "Camp" books:

> 2000 Camp Meeting – The Power Of God's Word In The Science Of Faith
>
> 2001 Camp Meeting – God's Character, The Best News In The Universe
>
> 2002 Camp Meeting – The Powerful Message Of The Two Covenants
>
> 2003 Camp Meeting – Elect According To The Foreknowledge of God
>
> And now:
>
> 2004 Camp Meeting – The Proclamation of the Acceptable Year of the Lord

These lectures include studies on the Harvest Principle and the Generation Concept. They show why we are now again in the time when all heaven is waiting to be gracious so as to enable Christ's wife to make herself ready!

> "The time has come when we must expect the Lord to do great things for us. Our efforts must not flag or weaken. We are to grow in grace and in the knowledge of the Lord. Before the work is closed up and the sealing of God's people is finished, we shall receive the outpouring of the Spirit of God. Angels from heaven will be in our midst. The present is a fitting-up time for heaven when we must walk in full obedience to all the commands of God." 1SM 111

Let us pray earnestly for the revival and reformation we so desperately need!

Dr. Elliot O. Douglin
August 2004

Table of

Contents

Introduction

Nearness of the End
E.G. White – Review and Herald March 14, 1912

"Troublous times are right upon us. The fulfilling of the signs of the times gives evidence that the day of the Lord is near at hand. The daily papers are full of indications of a terrible conflict in the future. Bold robberies are of frequent occurrence. Strikes are common. Thefts and murders are committed on every hand. Men possessed of demons are taking the lives of men and women and little children. All these things testify that the coming of Christ is near at hand.

"The doctrine that men are released from obedience to God's requirements has weakened the force of moral obligation, and opened the flood-gates of iniquity upon the world. Lawlessness, dissipation and corruption are sweeping upon us like an overwhelming tide. In the family, Satan is at work. His banner waves even in professedly Christian households. There is envy, evil surmising, hypocrisy, strife, betrayal of sacred trusts, indulgence of lust. The whole system of religious principles and doctrines, which should form the foundation and framework of social life, seems to be a tottering mass, ready to fall to ruin.

"Courts of justice are corrupt. Rulers are actuated by a desire for gain, and love of sensual pleasure. Intemperance has beclouded the faculties of many, so that Satan has almost complete control of them. Jurists are perverted, bribed, deluded. Drunkenness and revelry, passion, envy, dishonesty of every sort, are represented among those who administer the laws. "Justice standeth afar off: for truth is fallen in the street, and equity can not enter." Men are rushing on in the mad race for gain and selfish indulgence as if there were no God, no heaven, and no hereafter.

"The Scriptures describe the condition of the world just before Christ's second coming. The apostle James pictures the greed and oppression that will prevail. He says: "Go to now, ye rich men, . . . ye have heaped treasure together for the last days. Behold, the hire of the laborers who have reaped down your fields, which is of you kept back by fraud, crieth: and the cries of them which have reaped are entered into the ears of the Lord of Sabaoth. Ye have lived in pleasure on the earth, and been wanton. Ye have nourished your hearts, as in a day of slaughter. Ye have condemned and killed the just; and he doth not resist you." This is a picture of what exists to-day. By every species of oppression and extortion, men are piling up colossal fortunes, while the cries of starving humanity are coming up before God.

"In accidents and calamities by land and by sea, in great conflagrations, in fierce tornadoes and terrific hail-storms, in tempests, floods, cyclones, tidal waves, and earthquakes,–in every place and in a thousand forms, Satan is exercising his power. He sweeps away the ripening harvest, and famine and distress follow. He imparts to the air a deadly taint, and thousands perish by the pestilence. These visitations are to become more and more frequent and disastrous. Destruction will be upon both man and beast. "The earth mourneth and fadeth away, . . . the haughty people of the earth do languish. The earth also is defiled under the inhabitants thereof; because they have transgressed the laws, changed the ordinance, broken the everlasting covenant." Isaiah 24:4,5

"The crisis is stealing gradually upon us. The sun shines in the heavens, passing over its usual round, and the heavens still declare the glory of God. Men are still eating and drinking, planting and building, marrying and giving in marriage. Merchants are still buying and selling. Men are jostling against one another, contending for the highest place. Pleasure lovers are still crowding to theaters, horse-races, gambling-hells. The highest excitement prevails, yet probation's hour is fast closing, and every case is about to be eternally decided. Satan sees that his time is short. He has set all his agents to work, that men may be deceived, deluded, occupied, and entranced, until the day of probation shall be ended, and the door of mercy be forever shut. The time is right upon us when there will be sorrow that no human balm can heal. Sentinel angels are now restraining the four winds, that they shall not blow till the servants of God are sealed in their foreheads; but when God shall bid his angels loose the winds, there will be a scene of strife such as no pen can picture.

"The "time of trouble, such as never was," is soon to open upon us; and we shall need an experience which many are too indolent to obtain. It is often the case that trouble is greater in anticipation than in reality, but this is not true of the crisis before us. The most vivid presentation cannot reach the magnitude of the ordeal. In that trial every man must stand for himself before God. Though Noah, Daniel, and Job were in the land, "as I live, saith the Lord God, they shall deliver neither sons nor daughters;" "they should deliver but their own souls by their righteousness."

"Now, while our great High Priest is making the atonement for us, we should seek to become perfect in Christ. Not even by a thought could our Saviour be brought to yield to the power of temptation. Satan finds in human hearts some point where he can gain a foothold; some sinful desire is cherished, by means of which his temptations assert their power. But Christ declared of himself, "The prince of this world cometh, and hath nothing in me." Satan could find nothing in the Son of God that would enable him to gain the victory. He had kept his Father's commandments, and there was no sin in him that Satan could use to his advantage. This is the condition in which those must be found who shall stand in the time of trouble.

"Our God shall come, and shall not keep silence: a fire shall devour before him, and it shall be very tempestuous round about him. He shall call to the heavens from above, and to the earth, that he may judge his people. Gather my saints together unto me; those that have made a covenant with me by sacrifice. And the heavens shall declare his righteousness: for God is judge himself." (Ps 50: 3-6) RH 3-14-1912

1 The Harvest Principle and the Second Coming of Christ

As Seventh Day Adventists we have been looking for the imminent return of our Lord Jesus Christ ever since the earliest years of the proclamation of the First Angel's message during the period 1831 to 1844. The years have rolled on since that time and we are still looking for, and preaching the doctrine of, the Second Coming of Christ. And this we must continue to do!

But there is a principle many overlook, some reject it, while others have never even heard of it! We are talking about the **harvest principle**. What is the **harvest principle**?

> *"And he said, So is the kingdom of God, as if a man should cast seed into the ground; And should sleep, and rise night and day, and the seed should spring and grow up, he knoweth not how. For the earth bringeth forth fruit of herself; first the blade, then the ear, after that the full corn in the ear. But when the fruit is brought forth, immediately he putteth in the sickle, because the harvest is come."*
> *Mark 4:26-29*

Jesus will **not** come again until the harvest is ripe! Let us now read Revelation 14:14-16:

"And I looked, and behold a white cloud, and upon the cloud one sat like unto the Son of man, having on his head a golden crown, and in his hand a sharp sickle. And another angel came out of the temple, crying with a loud voice to him that sat on the cloud, Thrust in thy sickle, and reap: for the time is come for thee to reap; for the harvest of the earth is ripe. And he that sat on the cloud thrust in his sickle on the earth; and the earth was reaped." Rev 14:14-16

The word of God is clear that when the **harvest of the earth is ripe it will be time for Christ to return to reap the harvest**. He will not come a minute earlier or later but at the exact time that the harvest is ripe and ready! Jesus explains in Matthew Ch. 13 that the harvest is the end of the world.

"He answered and said unto them, He that soweth the good seed is the Son of man; The field is the world; the good seed are the children of the kingdom; but the tares are the children of the wicked one ; The enemy that sowed them is the devil; the harvest is the end of the world; and the reapers are the angels. As therefore the tares are gathered and burned in the fire; so shall it be in the end of this world. The Son of man shall send forth his angels, and they shall gather out of his kingdom all things that offend, and them which do iniquity; And shall cast them into a furnace of fire: there shall be wailing and gnashing of teeth. Then shall the righteous shine forth as the sun in the kingdom of their Father. Who hath ears to hear, let him hear." Matthew 13:37-43

Remember now we are discussing the harvest of righteousness.

What Is Meant By Being Harvest Ripe?

The Apostle Paul answers clearly in Ephesians Chapter 4. Paul is discussing why the risen and ascended Lord Jesus Christ gave (and gives) certain offices to the church.

"And he gave some, apostles; and some, prophets; and some, evangelists; and some, pastors and teachers; For the perfecting of the saints, for the work of the ministry, for the edifying of the body of Christ: Till we all come in the unity of the faith, and of the knowledge of the Son of God, unto a perfect man,

unto the measure of the stature of the fullness of Christ: That we henceforth be no more children, tossed to and fro, and carried about with every wind of doctrine, by the sleight of men, and cunning craftiness, whereby they lie in wait to deceive; But speaking the truth in love, may grow up into him in all things, which is the head, even Christ:" Eph 4:11-15

Paul employs a number of terms to describe the ultimate maturity to which Christ must bring His remnant church in the end-time. Let us examine these terms concisely.

1 — Unity Of Faith

First of all the harvest ripe church will have come into unity of the faith and of the knowledge of the Son of God (verse 13). There will no longer be a number of theories on the human nature of Christ when He was here on earth, rather the harvest ripe remnant people of God will be united in the one true doctrine of the kind of human nature the Son of God took on in His incarnation. Moreover, the knowledge of the Son of God means the true understanding of the true gospel. Such a knowledge along with the true doctrine of Christ's earthly human nature was certainly contained in the Jones-Waggoner 1888-1901 message on the covenants and righteousness by faith.

2 — The Measure Of The Stature Of The Fullness Of Christ

In Ephesians 4:13 Paul uses the term "perfect man" and immediately explains this as coming unto "the measure of the stature of the fullness of Christ." This refers to the full reproduction of the character of Christ in the harvest-ripe end-time believer.

> *"My little children, of whom I travail in birth again until Christ be formed in you," Galatians 4:19*

The term **"the full corn in the ear"** means the same as **"the measure of the stature of the fullness of Christ."**

> *"The fruit of the Spirit is love, joy, peace, longsuffering, gentleness, goodness, faith, meekness, temperance."* Gal. 5: 22, 23. This fruit can never perish, but will produce after

its kind a harvest unto eternal life. *"When the fruit is brought forth, immediately he putteth in the sickle, because the harvest is come."* Christ is waiting with longing desire for the manifestation of Himself in His church. When the character of Christ shall be perfectly reproduced in His people, then He will come to claim them as His own.."
C.O.L 69

"Of the Spirit Jesus said, *"He shall glorify Me."* The Saviour came to glorify the Father by the demonstration of His love; so the Spirit was to glorify Christ by revealing His grace to the world. The very image of God is to be reproduced in humanity. The honor of God, the honor of Christ, is involved in the perfection of the character of His people." D.A 671

3 — Not Tossed To And Fro

Thirdly Paul emphasizes in verse 14 the fact that the victorious end-time people of God will be so completely settled into the truth that they will not be "tossed to and fro" or "carried about with every wind of doctrine." Sanctified by the truth they will grow up into Christ in all things!

> *"To the law and to the testimony: if they speak not according to this word, it is because there is no light in them."* Isaiah 8:20. The people of God are directed to the Scriptures as their safeguard against the influence of false teachers and the delusive power of spirits of darkness. Satan employs every possible device to prevent men from obtaining a knowledge of the Bible; for its plain utterances reveal his deceptions. At every revival of God's work the prince of evil is aroused to more intense activity; he is now putting forth his utmost efforts for a final struggle against Christ and His followers. The last great delusion is soon to open before us. Antichrist is to perform his marvelous works in our sight. So closely will the counterfeit resemble the true that it will be impossible to distinguish between them except by the Holy Scriptures. By their testimony every statement and every miracle must be tested.

"Those who endeavor to obey all the commandments of God will be opposed and derided. They can stand only in God. In order to endure the trial before them, they must understand the will of God as revealed in His word; they can honor Him only as they have a right conception of His character, government, and purposes, and act in accordance with them. None but those who have fortified the mind with the truths of the Bible will stand through the last great conflict. To every soul will come the searching test: Shall I obey God rather than men? The decisive hour is even now at hand. Are our feet planted on the rock of God's immutable word? Are we prepared to stand firm in defense of the commandments of God and the faith of Jesus?

"But God will have a people upon the earth to maintain the Bible, and the Bible only, as the standard of all doctrines and the basis of all reforms. The opinions of learned men, the deductions of science, the creeds or decisions of ecclesiastical councils, as numerous and discordant as are the churches which they represent, the voice of the majority–not one nor all of these should be regarded as evidence for or against any point of religious faith. Before accepting any doctrine or precept, we should demand a plain "Thus saith the Lord" in its support. G.C 593-595

What Is Necessary To Ripen the Harvest?

The answer is given in James 5:7,8:

> *"Be patient therefore, brethren, unto the coming of the Lord. Behold, the husbandman waiteth for the precious fruit of the earth, and hath long patience for it, until he receive the early and latter rain. Be ye also patient; stablish your hearts: for the coming of the Lord draweth nigh." James 5:7,8*

While both the **early** and the **latter** rain of the Holy Spirit are required to produce a truly harvest-ripe end-time church, it is specifically the latter rain which ripens the harvest for the Second Coming of Jesus:

"Sow to yourselves in righteousness, reap in mercy; break up your fallow ground: for it is time to seek the LORD, till he come and rain righteousness upon you." Hosea 10:12

"Then shall we know, if we follow on to know the LORD: his going forth is prepared as the morning; and he shall come unto us as the rain, as the latter and former rain unto the earth." Hosea 6:3

"Ask ye of the LORD rain in the time of the latter rain; so the LORD shall make bright clouds, and give them showers of rain, to every one grass in the field." Zech 10:1

"Be glad then, ye children of Zion, and rejoice in the LORD your God: for he hath given you the former rain moderately, and he will cause to come down for you the rain, the former rain, and the latter rain in the first month." Joel 2:23

"In the East the former rain falls at the sowing time. It is necessary in order that the seed may germinate. Under the influence of the fertilizing showers, the tender shoot springs up. The latter rain, falling near the close of the season, ripens the grain and prepares it for the sickle. The Lord employs these operations of nature to represent the work of the Holy Spirit. As the dew and the rain are given first to cause the seed to germinate, and then to ripen the harvest, so the Holy Spirit is given to carry forward, from one stage to another, the process of spiritual growth. The ripening of the grain represents the completion of the work of God's grace in the soul. By the power of the Holy Spirit the moral image of God is to be perfected in the character. We are to be wholly transformed into the likeness of Christ.

"The latter rain, ripening earth's harvest, represents the spiritual grace that prepares the church for the coming of the Son of man. But unless the former rain has fallen, there will be no life; the green blade will not spring up. Unless the early showers have done their work, the latter rain can bring no seed to perfection.

"There is to be *'first the blade, then the ear, after that the full corn in the ear.'* There must be a constant development of Christian virtue, a constant advancement in Christian experience. This we should seek with intensity of desire, that we may adorn the doctrine of Christ our Saviour.

"Many have in a great measure failed to receive the former rain. They have not obtained all the benefits that God has thus provided for them. They expect that the lack will be supplied by the latter rain. When the richest abundance of grace shall be bestowed, they intend to open their hearts to receive it. They are making a terrible mistake. The work that God has begun in the human heart in giving His light and knowledge must be continually going forward. Every individual must realize his own necessity. The heart must be emptied of every defilement and cleansed for the indwelling of the Spirit. It was by the confession and forsaking of sin, by earnest prayer and consecration of themselves to God, that the early disciples prepared for the outpouring of the Holy Spirit on the Day of Pentecost. The same work, only in greater degree, must be done now. Then the human agent had only to ask for the blessing, and wait for the Lord to perfect the work concerning him. It is God who began the work, and He will finish His work, making man complete in Jesus Christ. But there must be no neglect of the grace represented by the former rain. Only those who are living up to the light they have will receive greater light. Unless we are daily advancing in the exemplification of the active Christian virtues, we shall not recognize the manifestations of the Holy Spirit in the latter rain. It may be falling on hearts all around us, but we shall not discern or receive it.

"At no point in our experience can we dispense with the assistance of that which enables us to make the first start. The blessings received under the former rain are needful to us to the end. Yet these alone will not suffice. While we cherish the blessings of the early rain, we must not, on the other hand, lose sight of the fact that without the latter rain, to fill out the ears and ripen the grain, the harvest will

not be ready for the sickle, and the labor of the sower will
have been in vain. Divine grace is needed at the beginning,
divine grace at every step of advance, and divine grace
alone can complete the work. There is no place for us
to rest in a careless attitude. We must never forget the
warnings of Christ, "Watch unto prayer," "Watch, . . . and
pray always." A connection with the divine agency every
moment is essential to our progress. We may have had a
measure of the Spirit of God, but by prayer and faith we
are continually to seek more of the Spirit. It will never do to
cease our efforts. If we do not progress, if we do not place
ourselves in an attitude to receive both the former and the
latter rain, we shall lose our souls, and the responsibility
will lie at our own door." T.M 506

The ministration of Christ, our High Priest, in the First Apartment
of the Heavenly Sanctuary (31 A.D. to 1844 A.D.) was the Early Rain
dispensation for the historic Church of Christ. The Latter Rain
dispensation commenced in 1844 at the close of the 2300 day–years
of Daniel 8:14. Our High Priest is now in the Most Holy Place of
the Heavenly sanctuary where He is doing the most holy work of
perfecting His remnant for the final crisis and the end of the world.

   In Revelation 14:6-12 there is the description of the three angels'
messages followed immediately by a description of the Son of
man coming with the sickle in His hand. It should be clearly seen
therefore that the three angels' messages (all comprehended
in the third) constitute the latter rain truth which ripens the
remnant for the harvest.

"The latter rain, ripening earth's harvest, represents the
spiritual grace that prepares the church for the coming of
the Son of Man." T.M. 506

"To prepare a people to stand in the day of God, a great work
of reform was to be accomplished. God saw that many of
His professed people were not building for eternity, and
in His mercy He was about to send a message of warning
to arouse them from their stupor and lead them to make
ready for the coming of the Lord.

"This warning is brought to view in Revelation 14. Here is a threefold message represented as proclaimed by heavenly beings and immediately followed by the coming of the Son of man to reap *'the harvest of the earth.'*" G.C. 311

"The third angel, flying in the midst of heaven and heralding the commandments of God and the testimony of Jesus, represents our work. The message loses none of its force in the angel's onward flight, for John sees it increasing in strength and power until the whole earth is lightened with its glory. The course of God's commandment-keeping people is onward, ever onward. The message of truth that we bear must go to nations, tongues, and peoples. Soon it will go with a loud voice, and the earth will be lightened with its glory. Are we preparing for this great outpouring of the Spirit of God?" 5T 383

Application To The Individual Believer

The work of **ripening** a final generation believer **begins** at conversion and will **end** at perfection of character. There is to be *"first the blade, then the ear, after that the full corn in the ear."* The "blade" or germination represents the beginning of spiritual life. The "ear" represents the entering into that **permanence** of surrender which signals entire consecration and full commitment to allow the Lord Jesus by His Spirit to fully reproduce His character in the believer. The ripening of the grain represents the completion of the work of God's grace in the soul. By the power of the Holy Spirit the moral image of God is to be perfected in the character. The end-time believer is to be wholly transformed into the likeness of Christ.

What Ripening Entails

"Having therefore these promises, dearly beloved, let us cleanse ourselves from all filthiness of the flesh and spirit, perfecting holiness in the fear of God." 2 Cor 7:1

"He that covereth his sins shall not prosper: but whoso confesseth and forsaketh them shall have mercy." Proverbs 28:13.

"If those who hide and excuse their faults could see how Satan exults over them, how he taunts Christ and holy angels with their course, they would make haste to confess their sins and to put them away. Through defects in the character, Satan works to gain control of the whole mind, and he knows that if these defects are cherished, he will succeed. Therefore he is constantly seeking to deceive the followers of Christ with his fatal sophistry that it is impossible for them to overcome. But Jesus pleads in their behalf His wounded hands, His bruised body; and He declares to all who would follow Him: *'My grace is sufficient for thee.'* 2 Corinthians 12:9. *'Take My yoke upon you, and learn of Me; for I am meek and lowly in heart: and ye shall find rest unto your souls. For My yoke is easy, and My burden is light.'* Matthew 11:29, 30. Let none, then, regard their defects as incurable. God will give faith and grace to overcome them." G.C 489

Ripening entails overcoming all deep-seated defects of character and being filled with the fruits of the Spirit.

"But the fruit of the Spirit is love, joy, peace, longsuffering, gentleness, goodness, faith, Meekness, temperance: against such there is no law." Gal 5:22,23

"This union with Christ, once formed, must be maintained. Christ said, *'Abide in Me, and I in you. As the branch cannot bear fruit of itself, except it abide in the vine; no more can ye, except ye abide in Me.'* This is no casual touch, no off-and-on connection. The branch becomes a part of the living vine. The communication of life, strength, and fruitfulness from the root to the branches is unobstructed and constant. Separated from the vine, the branch cannot live. No more, said Jesus, can you live apart from Me. The life you have received from Me can be preserved only by continual communion. Without Me you cannot overcome one sin, or resist one temptation.

"'Abide in Me, and I in you.' Abiding in Christ means a constant receiving of His Spirit, a life of unreserved

surrender to His service. The channel of communication must be open continually between man and his God. As the vine branch constantly draws the sap from the living vine, so are we to cling to Jesus, and receive from Him by faith the strength and perfection of His own character.

"The root sends its nourishment through the branch to the outermost twig. So Christ communicates the current of spiritual strength to every believer. So long as the soul is united to Christ, there is no danger that it will wither or decay.

"The life of the vine will be manifest in fragrant fruit on the branches. *'He that abideth in Me,'* said Jesus, *'and I in him, the same bringeth forth much fruit: for without Me ye can do nothing.'* When we live by faith on the Son of God, the fruits of the Spirit will be seen in our lives; not one will be missing.

"*'My Father is the husbandman. Every branch in Me that beareth not fruit He taketh away.'* While the graft is outwardly united with the vine, there may be no vital connection. Then there will be no growth or fruitfulness. So there may be an apparent connection with Christ without a real union with Him by faith. A profession of religion places men in the church, but the character and conduct show whether they are in connection with Christ. If they bear no fruit, they are false branches. Their separation from Christ involves a ruin as complete as that represented by the dead branch. *'If a man abide not in Me,'* said Christ, *'he is cast forth as a branch, and is withered; and men gather them, and cast them into the fire, and they are burned.'*" D.A 676

"*'Herein is My Father glorified,'* said Jesus, *'that ye bear much fruit.'* God desires to manifest through you the holiness, the benevolence, the compassion, of His own character. Yet the Saviour does not bid the disciples labor to bear fruit. He tells them to abide in Him. *'If ye abide in Me,'* He says, *'and My words abide in you, ye shall ask what ye will, and it shall be done unto you.'* It is through the word that Christ abides in His followers. This is the same vital union that is represented by eating His flesh and drinking His blood. The words of Christ are spirit and life. Receiving them, you receive the life of the Vine. You live *'by every word that proceedeth out of the mouth of God.'* Matt. 4:4. The life of Christ in you produces the same fruits as in Him. Living in Christ, adhering to Christ, supported by Christ, drawing nourishment from Christ, you bear fruit after the similitude of Christ." DA 677

The Apocalyptic Description Of The Harvest-Ripe Remnant

The book of Revelation describes the remnant church of God as keepers of the commandments of God and the faith of Jesus. (Rev. 14:12) The ten–commandment moral law of God is a description of God's character. But where it reveals God's character, it exposes human failure. It points out our sin.

Sin is defined in 1 John 3:4 as the transgression of the moral law. Sin is also defined in Romans 3:23 as falling short of the glory of God. If sin is breaking the law and sin is also falling short of the God's glory it should be clear that the law of God is a transcript of His glory. By the glory of God is meant His character.

The law reveals the character, the righteousness, of God. The law exposes our failure. But the most important function of the law is that of bringing us to Christ to be justified and to have the righteousness of the law, the character of God, fulfilled in us!

The keeping of the commandments and the faith of Jesus means the full reproduction of the character of God in the believer, in and through Christ by the Holy Spirit.

In addition to all the fundamental Seventh Day Adventist doctrines there are two ripening doctrines necessary for perfection of character. These are (i) the glorious truth of righteousness by faith – Christ our righteousness and (ii) the glorious message of the character of God.

Adventists should never forget the importance of Health Reform in the preparation of God's people for the coming of the Lord.

See additional text, Appendix A, page 208.

2 Why the Time of the Second Coming of Christ Is Not Revealed

"But of that day and hour knoweth no man, no, not the angels of heaven, but my Father only." Matthew 24:36

God has not arbitrarily set a preordained time for any of the terminal events. He has set the condition but not the time. The condition, as we have already seen in Chapter One, is stated in Mark 4:26-29. When the "harvest" is ready then and only then will Jesus return! Or to make it even clearer, "When the character of Christ shall be fully reproduced in His people then He will come to claim them as His own." C.O.L. 69

Now it should be obvious that God the Father in His omniscience and foreknowledge knows, and has always known eternally, the exact time when the harvest will be ready and therefore the exact time of the Second Advent.

But not only has God **not** set any arbitrary time for the Second Advent but He has also chosen **not** to reveal the time (which He foreknows) before the harvest is ripe.

Because to reveal the time would defeat His very purpose of allowing His people to mature in the divine character as quickly as they freely choose to mature under the motivation of His eternal Agapé love without a time-table being imposed upon them from without!

God wants His people to determine their own velocity of growth, a velocity which is as fast as their reception of, and response to, His love revealed in the Plan of Salvation centered in the infinite sacrifice of His Son! It is for these reasons that the inspired word tells us that it is our privilege not only to look for but to hasten the coming of the Lord!

> *"But the day of the Lord will come as a thief in the night; in the which the heavens shall pass away with a great noise, and the elements shall melt with fervent heat, the earth also and the works that are therein shall be burned up. Seeing then that all these things shall be dissolved, what manner of persons ought ye to be in all holy conversation and godliness, Looking for and hasting unto the coming of the day of God, wherein the heavens being on fire shall be dissolved, and the elements shall melt with fervent heat?" 2 Peter 3:10-12*

> "It is the privilege of every Christian not only to look for but to hasten the coming of our Lord Jesus Christ.' (2 Peter 3:12, margin). Were all who profess His name bearing fruit to His glory, how quickly the whole world would be sown with the seed of the gospel. Quickly the last great harvest would be ripened, and Christ would come to gather the precious grain." C.O.L. 69

Times And Seasons

The disciples, after Christ's resurrection, wanted to know the time for the setting up of the kingdom and so they asked Jesus. He answered by informing them that what they needed was not a knowledge of the time when the kingdom would be set up but rather the power of the Holy Spirit to be effective witnesses for Him obviously by revealing His righteousness in word and lifestyle!

> *"They therefore, when they were come together, asked him, saying, Lord, dost thou at this time restore the kingdom to Israel? And he said unto them, It is not for you to know times or seasons, which the Father hath set within His own authority. But ye shall receive power, when the Holy Spirit*

*is come upon you: and ye shall be my witnesses both in
Jerusalem, and in all Judaea and Samaria, and unto the
uttermost part of the earth." Acts 1:6-8 ASV*

In Acts 1:7 Jesus said that it is not for us to know the times or
seasons which the Father has put in His own power. And yet in 1
Thessalonians 5:1, Paul told the Thessalonians that there was no
need to write to them about times and seasons. He was obviously
implying that they already knew about such times and seasons.
Was Paul contradicting Jesus? No!

Those "times and seasons" which define the **time** of the Second
Coming are **not** for us to know. Those "times and seasons" which
define the **nearness** of the end, and the urgency of preparation,
are for us to know.

This is confirmed in Matthew 24:3, where the disciples asked
what shall be the sign of His coming and He answered them by de-
scribing the events which would indicate the nearness of the end.

And of course in Matthew 24:33-34 Jesus settled the matter.
Knowing the indicators of the nearness of the end is not setting
a date for the end. Similarly, the appreciation of generational
urgency is not setting a date for the end.

> *"...even so ye also, when ye see all these things, know ye
> that he is nigh, even at the doors. Verily I say unto you,
> This generation shall not pass away, till all these things be
> accomplished." Matt 24:33-34*

Ours Is Not A Time-Setting Message

> "We are not of that class who define the exact period of time
> that shall elapse before the coming of Jesus the second
> time with power and great glory. Some have set a time, and
> when that has passed, their presumptuous spirits have not
> accepted rebuke, but they have set another and another
> time. But many successive failures have stamped them as
> false prophets.—FE 335 (1895).

> "God gives no man a message that it will be five years
> or ten years or twenty years before this earth's history
> shall close. He would not give any living being an excuse

for delaying the preparation for His appearing. He would have no one say, as did the unfaithful servant, "My lord delayeth his coming," for this leads to reckless neglect of the opportunities and privileges given to prepare us for that great day.—RH Nov. 27, 1900.

Time-setting Leads to Unbelief

"Because the times repeatedly set have passed, the world is in a more decided state of unbelief than before in regard to the near advent of Christ. They look upon the failures of the time-setters with disgust, and because men have been so deceived, they turn from the truth substantiated by the Word of God that the end of all things is at hand.— 4T 307 (1879).

"I understand that Brother [E. P.] Daniels has, as it were, set time, stating that the Lord will come within five years. Now I hope the impression will not go abroad that we are time-setters. Let no such remarks be made. They do no good. Seek not to obtain a revival upon any such grounds, but let due caution be used in every word uttered, that fanatical ones will not seize anything they can get to create an excitement and the Spirit of the Lord be grieved.

"We want not to move the people's passions to get up a stir, where feelings are moved and principle does not control. I feel that we need to be guarded on every side, because Satan is at work to do his uttermost to insinuate his arts and devices that shall be a power to do harm. Anything that will make a stir, create an excitement on a wrong basis, is to be dreaded, for the reaction will surely come.— Letter 34, 1887.

"There will always be false and fanatical movements made by persons in the church who claim to be led of God— those who will run before they are sent and will give day and date for the occurrence of unfulfilled prophecy. The enemy is pleased to have them do this, for their successive failures and leading into false lines cause confusion and unbelief.—2SM 84 (1897).

No Time Prophecy Beyond 1844

"I plainly stated at the Jackson camp meeting to these fanatical parties that they were doing the work of the adversary of souls; they were in darkness. They claimed to have great light that probation would close in October, 1884. I there stated in public that the Lord had been pleased to show me that there would be no definite time in the message given of God since 1844.—2SM 73 (1885).

"Our position has been one of waiting and watching, with no time-proclamation to intervene between the close of the prophetic periods in 1844 and the time of our Lord's coming.—10MR 270 (1888).

"The people will not have another message upon definite time. After this period of time [Rev. 10:4-6], reaching from 1842 to 1844, there can be no definite tracing of the prophetic time. The longest reckoning reaches to the autumn of 1844.—7BC 971 (1900)." Last Day Events 34, 35

"But if that evil servant shall say in his heart, My lord tarrieth; and shall begin to beat his fellow-servants, and shall eat and drink with the drunken; the lord of that servant shall come in a day when he expecteth not, and in an hour when he knoweth not, and shall cut him asunder, and appoint his portion with the hypocrites: there shall be the weeping and the gnashing of teeth." Matt 24:48-51

What Christ Is Waiting For

"Christ is waiting with longing desire for the manifestation of Himself in His church. When the character of Christ shall be perfectly reproduced in His people, then He will come to claim them as His own.

"It is the privilege of every Christian, not only to look for, but to hasten the coming of our Lord Jesus Christ. Were all who profess His name bearing fruit to His glory, how quickly the whole world would be sown with the seed of the gospel. Quickly the last great harvest would be ripened, and Christ would come to gather the precious grain.—COL 69 (1900).

"By giving the gospel to the world it is in our power to hasten our Lord's return. We are not only to look for but to hasten the coming of the day of God (2 Peter 3:12, margin).—DA 633 (1898).

"He has put it in our power, through cooperation with Him, to bring this scene of misery to an end.— Ed 264 (1903). Last Day Events 39

Appeal

"May the Lord give no rest, day nor night, to those who are now careless and indolent in the cause and work of God. The end is near. This is that which Jesus would have us keep ever before us the shortness of time." Letter 97, 1886. Last Day Events 42

3 It Is Not For You to Know the Times and the Seasons

(E.G. White: Review and Herald, March 22, 1892)

"He showed himself alive after his passion by many infallible proofs, being seen of them forty days, and speaking of the things pertaining to the kingdom of God: and, being assembled together with them, commanded them that they should not depart from Jerusalem, but wait for the promise of the Father, which, saith he, ye have heard of me. For John truly baptized with water; but ye shall be baptized with the Holy Ghost not many days hence. When they therefore were come together, they asked of him, saying, Lord, wilt thou at this time restore again the kingdom to Israel? And he said unto them, It is not for you to know the times or the seasons, which the Father hath put in his own power." Acts 1:3-7

"The disciples were anxious to know the exact time for the revelation of the kingdom of God; but Jesus tells them that they may not know the times and the seasons; for the Father has not revealed them. To understand when the kingdom of God should be restored, was not the thing of most importance for them to know. They were to be found following the Master, praying, waiting, watching, and working. They were to be representatives to the world of the character of Christ. That which was essential for a successful Christian experience in the days of the disciples, is essential in our day. *'And he said unto them, It is not for you to know the times or the seasons, which the Father hath put in his own power. But ye shall receive power, after that the Holy Ghost is come upon you.'* And after the Holy Ghost was come upon them, what were they to do? "And ye shall be witnesses unto me both in Jerusalem, and in all Judea, and in Samaria, and unto the uttermost parts of the earth."

"This is the work in which we also are to be engaged. Instead of living in expectation of some special season of excitement, we are wisely to improve present opportunities, doing that which must be done in order that souls may be saved. Instead of exhausting the powers of our mind in speculations in regard to the times and seasons which the Lord has placed in his own power, and withheld from men, we are to yield ourselves to the control of the Holy Spirit, to do present duties, to give the bread of life, unadulterated with human opinions, to souls who are perishing for the truth.

"Satan is ever ready to fill the mind with theories and calculations that will divert men from the present truth, and disqualify them for the giving of the third angel's message to the world. It has ever been thus; for our Saviour often had to speak reprovingly to those who indulged in speculations and were ever inquiring into those things which the Lord had not revealed. Jesus had come to earth to impart important truth to men, and he wished to impress their minds with the necessity of receiving and obeying his precepts and instructions, of doing their present duty, and his communications were of an order that imparted knowledge for their immediate and daily use.

"Jesus said: "This is life eternal, that they might know thee the only true God, and Jesus Christ, whom thou hast sent." All that was done and said had this one object in view,—to rivet truth in their minds that they might attain unto everlasting life. Jesus did not come to astonish men with some great announcement of some special time when some great event would occur, but he came to instruct and save the lost. He did not come to arouse and gratify curiosity; for he knew that this would but increase the appetite for the curious and the marvelous. It was his aim to impart knowledge whereby men might increase in spiritual strength, and advance in the way of obedience and true holiness. He gave only such instruction as could be appropriated to the needs of their daily life, only such truth as could be given to others for the same appropriation. He did not make new revelations to men, but opened to their understanding truths that had long been obscured or misplaced through the false teaching of the priests and teachers. Jesus replaced the gems of divine truth in their proper setting, in the order in which they had been given to patriarchs and prophets. And after giving them this precious instruction, he promised to give them the Holy Spirit whereby all things that he had said unto them should be brought to their remembrance.

"We are in continual danger of getting above the simplicity of the gospel. There is an intense desire on the part of many to startle the world with something original, that shall lift the people into a state of spiritual ecstasy, and change the present order of experience. There is certainly great need of a change in the present order of experience; for the sacredness of present truth is not realized as it should be, but the change we need is a change of heart, and can only be obtained by seeking God individually for his blessing, by pleading with him for his power, by fervently praying that his grace may come upon us, and that our characters may be transformed. This is the change we need to-day, and for the attainment of this experience we should exercise persevering energy and manifest heartfelt earnestness. We should ask with true sincerity, "What shall I do to be saved?" We should know just what steps we are taking heavenward.

"Christ gave to his disciples truths whose breadth and depth and value they little appreciated, or even comprehended, and the same condition exists among the people of God to-day. We too have failed to take in the greatness, to perceive the beauty of the truth which God has intrusted to us to-day. Should we advance in spiritual knowledge, we would see the truth developing and expanding in lines of which we have little dreamed, but it will never develop in any line that will lead us to imagine that we may know the times and the seasons which the Father hath put in his own power. Again and again have I been warned in regard to time-setting. There will never again be a message for the people of God that will be based on time. We are not to know the definite time either for the outpouring of the Holy Spirit or for the coming of Christ.

"I was searching through my writings, before coming to this meeting, to see what I should take with me to Australia, and I found an envelope on which was written, 'Testimony given in regard to time-setting, June 21, 1851. Preserve carefully.' I opened it, and this is what I found. It reads, 'A copy of a vision the Lord gave sister White June 21, 1851, at Camden, N. Y. The Lord showed me that the message must go, and that it must not be hung on time; for time will never be a test again. I saw that some were getting a false excitement, arising from preaching time, that the third angel's message can stand on its own foundation, and that it needs not time to strengthen it, and that it will go with mighty power, and do its work, and will be cut short in righteousness.

"'I saw some were making everything bend to this next fall; that is, making their calculations, and disposing of their property in reference to that time. I saw that this was wrong for this reason, instead of going to God daily, and earnestly desiring to know their present duty, they looked ahead, and made their calculations as though they knew that the work would end this fall, without inquiring their duty of God daily.' Copied at Milton, June 29, 1851. A. A. G.

"This was the document I came upon last Monday in searching over my writings, and here is another which was written in regard to a man who was setting time in 1884, and sending broadcast his arguments to prove his theories. The report of what he was doing was brought to me at the Jackson, Mich., camp-meeting, and I told the people they need not take heed to this man's theory; for the event he predicted would not take place. The times and the seasons God has put in his own power, and why has not God given us this knowledge?—*Because we would not make a right use of it if he did*. A condition of things would result from this knowledge among our people that would greatly retard the work of God in preparing a people to stand in the great day that is to come. *We are not to live upon time excitement.* We are not to be engrossed with speculations in regard to the times and the seasons which God has not revealed. Jesus has told his disciples to "watch," but not for definite time. His followers are to be in the position of those who are listening for the orders of their Captain; they are to watch, wait, pray, and work, as they approach the time for the coming of the Lord; but no one will be able to predict just when that time will come; for "of that day and hour knoweth no man." You will not be able to say that he will come in one, two, or five years, neither are you to put off his coming by stating that it may not be for ten or twenty years.

"It is the duty of the people of God to have their lamps trimmed and burning, to be as men that wait for the Bridegroom, when he shall return from the wedding. You have not a moment to lose in neglect of the great salvation that has been provided for you. The time of the probation of souls is coming to an end. From day to day the destiny of men is being sealed, and even from this congregation we know not how soon many shall close their eyes in death and be habited for the tomb. We should now consider that our life is swiftly passing away, that we are not safe one moment unless our life is hid with Christ in God. Our duty is not to be looking forward to some special time for some special work to be done for us, but to go forward in our work of warning the world; for we are to be witnesses of Christ to the uttermost parts of the world. All around us are the young, the impenitent, the unconverted, and what are we doing for them? Parents, in the ardor of your first love, are you seeking for the conversion of your children, or are you engrossed with the things of this life to such an extent that you are not making earnest efforts to be laborers together with God? Do you have an appreciation of the work and mission of the Holy Spirit? Do you realize that the Holy Spirit is the agency whereby we are to reach the souls of those around us? When this meeting shall close, will you go from here and forget the earnest appeals that have been made to you? will the messages of warning be left unheeded, and the truth you have heard leak out of your heart as water leaks out of a broken vessel?

"The apostle says, *'Therefore we ought to give the more earnest heed to the things which we have heard, lest at any time we should let them slip. For if the word spoken by angels was steadfast, and every transgression and disobedience received a just recompense of reward; how shall we escape, if we neglect so great salvation; which at the first began to be spoken by the Lord, and was confirmed unto us by them that heard him; God also bearing them witness, both with signs and wonders, and with divers miracles, and gifts of the Holy Ghost, according to his own will?'* Hebrews 2:1-4

"The third angel's message is swelling into a loud cry, and you must not feel at liberty to neglect the present duty, and still entertain the idea that at some future time you will be the recipients of great blessing, when without any effort on your part a wonderful revival will take place. To-day you are to give yourselves to God, that he may make of you vessels unto honor, and meet for his service. To-day you are to give yourself to God, that you may be emptied of self, emptied of envy, jealousy, evil-surmising, strife, everything that shall be dishonoring to God. To-day you are to have your vessel purified that it may be ready for the heavenly dew, ready for the showers of the latter rain; for the latter rain will come, and the blessing of God will fill every soul that is purified from every defilement. It is our work to-day to yield our souls to Christ, that we may be fitted for the time of refreshing from the presence of the Lord—fitted for the baptism of the Holy Spirit." RH 3-22-1892

4 Pray For the Latter Rain

(E.G. White: Review and Herald, March 2, 1897)

"'Ask ye of the Lord rain in the time of the latter rain; so the Lord shall make bright clouds, and give them showers of rain.' 'He will cause to come down for you the rain, the former rain, and the latter rain.' In the East the former rain falls at the sowing-time. It is necessary in order that the seed may germinate. Under the influence of the fertilizing showers, the tender shoot springs up. The latter rain, falling near the close of the season, ripens the grain, and prepares it for the sickle. The Lord employs these operations of nature to represent the work of the Holy Spirit. As the dew and the rain are given first to cause the seed to germinate, and then to ripen the harvest, so the Holy Spirit is given to carry forward, from one stage to another, the process of spiritual growth. The ripening of the grain represents the completion of the work of God's grace in

the soul. By the power of the Holy Spirit the moral image of God is to be perfected in the character. We are to be wholly transformed into the likeness of Christ.

"The latter rain, ripening earth's harvest, represents the spiritual grace that prepares the church for the coming of the Son of Man. But unless the former rain has fallen, there will be no life; the green blade will not spring up. Unless the early showers have done their work, the latter rain can bring no seed to perfection.

There is to be *'first the blade, then the ear, after that the full corn in the ear.'* There must be a constant development of Christian virtue, a constant advancement in Christian experience. This we should seek with intensity of desire, that we may adorn the doctrine of Christ our Saviour.

"Many have in a great measure failed to receive the former rain. They have not obtained all the benefits that God has thus provided for them. They expect that the lack will be supplied by the latter rain. When the richest abundance of grace shall be bestowed, they intend to open their hearts to receive it. They are making a terrible mistake. The work that God has begun in the human heart in giving his light and knowledge, must be continually going forward. Every individual must realize his own necessity. The heart must be emptied of every defilement, and cleansed for the indwelling of the Spirit. It was by the confession and forsaking of sin, by earnest prayer and consecration of themselves to God, that the early disciples prepared for the outpouring of the Holy Spirit on the day of Pentecost. The same work, only in greater degree, must be done now. Then the human agent had only to ask for the blessing, and wait for the Lord to perfect the work concerning him. It is God who began the work, and he will finish his work, making man complete in Jesus Christ. But there must be no neglect of the grace represented by the former rain. Only those who are living up to the light they have, will receive greater light. Unless we are daily advancing in the exemplification of the active Christian virtues, we shall not recognize the manifestations of the Holy Spirit in the latter rain. It may be falling on hearts all around us, but we shall not discern or receive it.

"At no point in our experience can we dispense with the assistance of that which enables us to make the first start. The blessings received under the former rain are needful to us to the end. Yet these alone will not suffice. While we cherish the blessing of the early rain, we must not, on the other hand, lose sight of the fact that without the latter rain, to fill out the ears and ripen the grain, the harvest will not be ready for the sickle, and the labor of the sower will have been in vain. Divine grace is needed at the beginning, divine grace at every step of advance, and divine grace alone can complete the work. There is no place for us to rest in a careless attitude. We must never forget the warnings of Christ, *'Watch unto prayer,' 'Watch and pray always.'* A connection with the divine agency every moment is essential to our progress. We may have had a measure of the Spirit of God, but by prayer and faith we are continually to seek more of the Spirit. It will never do to cease our efforts. If we do not progress, if we do not place ourselves in an attitude to receive both the former and the latter rain, we shall lose our souls, and the responsibility will lie at our own door.

"*'Ask ye of the Lord rain in the time of the latter rain.'* Do not rest satisfied that in the ordinary course of the season, rain will fall. Ask for it. The growth and perfection of the seed rests not with husbandman. God alone can ripen the harvest. But man's co-operation is required. God's work for us demands the action of our mind, the exercise of our faith. We must seek his favors with the whole heart if the showers of grace are to come to us. We should improve every opportunity of placing ourselves in the channel of blessing. Christ has said, *'Where two or three are gathered together in my name, there am I in the midst.'* The convocations of the church, as in camp-meetings, the assemblies of the home church, and all occasions where there is personal labor for souls, are God's appointed opportunities for giving the early and the latter rain.

"But let none think that in attending these gatherings, their duty is done. A mere attendance upon all the meetings that are held will not in itself bring a blessing to the soul. It is not an immutable law that all who attend general gatherings or local meetings shall receive large supplies from heaven. The circumstances may seem to be favorable for a rich outpouring of the showers of grace. But God himself must command the rain to fall. Therefore we should not be remiss in supplication. We are not to trust to the ordinary working of providence. We must pray that God will unseal the fountain of the water of life. And we must ourselves receive of the living water. Let us, with contrite hearts, pray most earnestly that now, in the time of the latter rain, the showers of grace may fall upon us. At every meeting we attend, our prayers should ascend that at this very time, God will impart warmth and moisture to our souls. As we seek God for the Holy Spirit, it will work in us meekness, humbleness of mind, a conscious dependence upon God for the perfecting latter rain. If we pray for the blessing in faith, we shall receive it as God has promised.

"The continual communication of the Holy Spirit to the church is represented by the prophet Zechariah under another figure, which contains a wonderful lesson of encouragement for us. The prophet says: *'The angel that talked with me came again, and waked me, as a man that is wakened out of his sleep, and said unto me, What seest thou? And I said, I have looked, and behold a candlestick all of gold, with a bowl upon the top of it, and his seven lamps thereon, and seven pipes to the seven lamps, which are upon the top thereof: and two olive-trees by it, one upon the right side of the bowl, and the other upon the left side thereof. So I answered and spake to the angel that talked with me, saying, What are these, my Lord?... Then he answered and spake unto me, saying, This is the word of the Lord unto Zerubbabel, saying, Not by might, nor by power, but by my Spirit, saith the Lord of Hosts. ...And I answered again, and said unto him, What be these two olive branches which through the two golden pipes empty the golden oil out of themselves?... Then said he, These are the two anointed ones, that stand by the Lord of the whole earth.'*

"From the two olive-trees, the golden oil was emptied through golden pipes into the bowl of the candlestick, and thence into the golden lamps that gave light to the sanctuary. So from the holy ones that stand in God's presence, his Spirit is imparted to human instrumentalities that are consecrated to his service. The mission of the two anointed ones is to communicate light and power to God's people. It is to receive blessing for us that they stand in God's presence. As the olive-trees empty themselves into the golden pipes, so the heavenly messengers seek to communicate all that they receive from God. The whole heavenly treasure awaits our demand and reception; and as we receive the blessing, we in our turn are to impart it. Thus it is that the holy lamps are fed, and the church becomes a light-bearer in the world.

"This is the work that the Lord would have every soul prepared to do at this time, when the four angels are holding the four winds, that they shall not blow until the servants of God are sealed in their foreheads. There is no time now for self-pleasing. The lamps of the soul must be trimmed. They must be supplied with the oil of grace. Every precaution must be taken to prevent spiritual declension, lest the great day of the Lord overtake us as a thief in the night. Every witness for God is now to work intelligently in the lines which God has appointed. We should daily obtain a deep and living experience in the work of perfecting Christian character. We should daily receive the holy oil that we may impart to others. All may be light-bearers to the world if they will. We are to sink self out of sight in Jesus. We are to receive the word of the Lord in counsel and instruction, and gladly communicate it. There is now need of much prayer. Christ commands, *'Pray without ceasing;'* that is, keep the mind uplifted to God, the source of all power and efficiency.

"We may have long followed the narrow path, but it is not safe to take this as proof that we shall follow it to the end. If we have walked with God in fellowship of the Spirit, it is because we have sought him daily by faith. From the two olive-trees, the golden oil flowing through the golden pipes has been communicated to us. *But those who do not cultivate the spirit and habit of prayer cannot expect to receive the golden oil of goodness, patience, long-suffering, gentleness, love.*

"Every one is to keep himself separate from the world, which is full of iniquity. We are not to walk with God for a time, and then part from his company, and walk in the sparks of our own kindling. There must be a firm continuance, a perseverance in acts of faith. We are to praise God, to show forth his glory in a righteous character. **No one of us will gain the victory without persevering, untiring effort, proportionate to the value of the object which we seek, even eternal life.**

"The dispensation in which we are now living is to be, to those that ask, the dispensation of the Holy Spirit. Ask for his blessing. It is time we were more intense in our devotion. To us is committed the arduous, but happy, glorious work of revealing Christ to those who are in darkness. We are called to proclaim the special truths for this time. For all this the outpouring of the Spirit is essential. We should pray for it. The Lord expects us to ask him. We have not been whole hearted in this work.

"What can I say to my brethren in the name of the Lord? What proportion of our efforts has been made in accordance with the light the Lord has been pleased to give. We cannot depend upon form or external machinery. What we need is the quickening influence of the Holy Spirit of God. *'Not by might, nor by power, but by my Spirit, saith the Lord of Hosts.'* Pray without ceasing, and watch by working in accordance with your prayers. As you pray, believe, trust in God. It is the time of the latter rain, when the Lord will give largely of his Spirit. Be fervent in prayer, and watch in the Spirit." RH 3-2-1897

5 Time Cycles In the Flow of History

Human history follows a cyclical pattern which reveals the outworking of certain mysterious principles. Generations come and go but there is a constancy and consistency about basic human response to basic issues in the great controversy.

Yet in the cycles of history the recurrent issues at stake have become more amplified in nature and more global in extent as time has passed over the six millennia of the history of the great controversy on this planet.

We say, in simple terms, that history repeats itself. But, in each repetition the conflict between right and wrong, truth and error, becomes more intense as it accelerates toward its inevitable climax.

There is a similarity between cycles in nature and cycles in history. The wise man Solomon gave much thought to these matters and actually wrote down some of his thoughts on the cycles in nature and in history in Ecclesiastes chapter 1:4-9. Notice his conclusion in verse 9:

> *"The thing that hath been, it is that which shall be; and that which is done is that which shall be done: and there is no new thing under the sun." Eccl 1:9*

Solomon explains this mystery further in Ecclesiastes 3:15:

> *"That which hath been is now; and that which is to be hath already been; and God requireth that which is past." Eccl 3:15*

Let us read two modern translations of this text:

> *"Whatever happens or can happen has already happened before. God makes the same thing happen again and again." Eccl 3:15 TEV*

> *"Whatever is, has been long ago; and whatever is going to be has been before; God brings to pass again what was in the past and disappeared." Eccl 3:15 LB*

But Solomon does not leave us there. He describes two very important basic principles which have always driven the cycles of history. One is the principle of **cause** and **effect**: *"the curse causeless shall not come."* The other is the principle that *"to every purpose there is* **time** *and* **judgement.***"*

> *"As the bird by wandering, as the swallow by flying, so the curse causeless shall not come." Proverbs 26:2*

> *"Whoso keepeth the commandment shall feel no evil thing: and a wise man's heart discerneth both time and judgment. Because to every purpose there is time and judgment, therefore the misery of man is great upon him." Eccles 8:5, 6*

These same principles are also expressed in the New Testament.

> *"Be not deceived; God is not mocked: for whatsoever a man soweth, that shall he also reap. For he that soweth to his flesh shall of the flesh reap corruption; but he that soweth to the Spirit shall of the Spirit reap life everlasting." Gal 6:7-9*

> *"Let no man say when he is tempted, I am tempted of God: for God cannot be tempted with evil, neither tempteth he any man: But every man is tempted, when he is drawn away of his own lust, and enticed. Then when lust hath conceived, it bringeth forth sin: and sin, when it is finished, bringeth forth death. Do not err, my beloved brethren.*

Every good gift and every perfect gift is from above, and cometh down from the Father of lights, with whom is no variableness, neither shadow of turning." James 1:13-17

These principles are especially applicable to religious history and specifically to **reformation**.

"The work of God in the earth presents, from age to age, a striking similarity in every great reformation or religious movement. The principles of God's dealing with men are ever the same. The important movements of the present have their parallel in those of the past, and the experience of the church in former ages has lessons of great value for our own time.

"No truth is more clearly taught in the Bible than that God by His Holy Spirit especially directs His servants on earth in the great movements for the carrying forward of the work of salvation. Men are instruments in the hand of God, employed by Him to accomplish His purposes of grace and mercy. Each has his part to act; to each is granted a measure of light, adapted to the necessities of his time, and sufficient to enable him to perform the work which God has given him to do. But no man, however honored of Heaven, has ever attained to a full understanding of the great plan of redemption, or even to a perfect appreciation of the divine purpose in the work for his own time. Men do not fully understand what God would accomplish by the work which He gives them to do; they do not comprehend, in all its bearings, the message which they utter in His name.

"'*Canst thou by searching find out God? canst thou find out the Almighty unto perfection?*' '*My thoughts are not your thoughts, neither are your ways My ways, saith the Lord. For as the heavens are higher than the earth, so are My ways higher than your ways, and My thoughts than your thoughts.*' '*I am God, and there is none like Me, declaring the end from the beginning, and from ancient times the things that are not yet done.*' Job 11:7; Isaiah 55:8, 9; 46:9, 10.

> "Even the prophets who were favored with the special illumination of the Spirit did not fully comprehend the import of the revelations committed to them. The meaning was to be unfolded from age to age, as the people of God should need the instruction therein contained." G.C 343,344

Since the principles of God's dealing with His people are ever the same we should study the following principle with an attitude of humility and repentance.

> "The Lord Jesus will always have a chosen people to serve Him. When the Jewish people rejected Christ, the Prince of life, He took from them the kingdom of God and gave it unto the Gentiles. God will continue to work on this principle with every branch of His work.

> "When a church proves unfaithful to the word of the Lord, whatever their position may be, however high and sacred their calling, the Lord can no longer work with them. Others are then chosen to bear important responsibilities. But, if these in turn do not purify their lives from every wrong action, if they do not establish pure and holy principles in all their borders, then the Lord will grievously afflict and humble them and, unless they repent, will remove them from their place and make them a reproach." 14MR 102 (1903).

These principles have also been at work in the rise and fall of the great empires of history.

> "In the annals of human history, the growth of nations, the rise and fall of empires, appear as if dependent on the will and prowess of man; the shaping of events seems, to a great degree, to be determined by his power, ambition, or caprice. But in the word of God the curtain is drawn aside, and we behold, above, behind, and through all the play and counterplay of human interest and power and passions, the agencies of the All-merciful One, silently, patiently working out the counsels of His own will." P.K 499, 500

> "In the history of nations the student of God's word may behold the literal fulfillment of divine prophecy. Babylon, shattered and broken at last, passed away because

in prosperity its rulers had regarded themselves as independent of God, and had ascribed the glory of their kingdom to human achievement. The Medo-Persian realm was visited by the wrath of Heaven because in it God's law had been trampled underfoot. The fear of the Lord had found no place in the hearts of the vast majority of the people. Wickedness, blasphemy, and corruption prevailed. The kingdoms that followed were even more base and corrupt; and these sank lower and still lower in the scale of moral worth." ibid 501, 502.

Since history is cyclical we can conclude that future events cast their shadows before. Or, to put it the other way, past events have been anticipatory or proleptic of future events. (In your group discussions work out the prolepsis of the Elijah, Jezebel story; the Babylon, Euphrates connection; Egypt in the O.T and Egypt in the Revelation.)

"Every nation that has come upon the stage of action has been permitted to occupy its place on the earth, that the fact might be determined whether it would fulfill the purposes of the Watcher and the Holy One. Prophecy has traced the rise and progress of the world's great empires–Babylon, Medo-Persia, Greece, and Rome. With each of these, as with the nations of less power, history has repeated itself. Each has had its period of test; each has failed, its glory faded, its power departed.

"While nations have rejected God's principles, and in this rejection have wrought their own ruin, yet a divine, overruling purpose has manifestly been at work throughout the ages. It was this that the prophet Ezekiel saw in the wonderful representation given him during his exile in the land of the Chaldeans, when before his astonished gaze were portrayed the symbols that revealed an overruling Power that has to do with the affairs of earthly rulers.

"Upon the banks of the river Chebar, Ezekiel beheld a whirlwind seeming to come from the north, *'a great cloud, and a fire infolding itself, and a brightness was about it, and out of the midst thereof as the color of amber.'* A number of wheels intersecting one another were moved by four living beings. High above all these *'was the likeness of a throne, as the appearance of a sapphire stone: and upon the likeness of the throne was the likeness as the appearance of a man above upon it.' 'And there appeared in the cherubims the form of a man's hand under their wings.'* Ezekiel 1:4, 26; 10:8. The wheels were so complicated in arrangement that at first sight they appeared to be in confusion; yet they moved in perfect harmony. Heavenly beings, sustained and guided by the hand beneath the wings of the cherubim, were impelling those wheels; above them, upon the sapphire throne, was the Eternal One; and round about the throne was a rainbow, the emblem of divine mercy.

"As the wheellike complications were under the guidance of the hand beneath the wings of the cherubim, so the complicated play of human events is under divine control. Amidst the strife and tumult of nations He that sitteth above the cherubim still guides the affairs of this earth.

"The history of nations speaks to us today. To every nation and to every individual God has assigned a place in His great plan. Today men and nations are being tested by the plummet in the hand of Him who makes no mistake. All are by their own choice deciding their destiny, and God is overruling all for the accomplishment of His purposes.

"The prophecies which the great I am has given in His word, uniting link after link in the chain of events, from eternity in the past to eternity in the future, tell us where we are today in the procession of the ages and what may be expected in the time to come. All that prophecy has foretold as coming to pass, until the present time, has been traced on the pages of history, and we may be assured that all which is yet to come will be fulfilled in its order.

"Today the signs of the times declare that we are standing on the threshold of great and solemn events. Everything in our world is in agitation. Before our eyes is fulfilling the Saviour's prophecy of the events to precede His coming: "Ye shall hear of wars and rumors of wars. . . . Nation shall rise against nation, and kingdom against kingdom: and there shall be famines, and pestilences, and earthquakes, in divers places." Matthew 24:6, 7.

"The present is a time of overwhelming interest to all living. Rulers and statesmen, men who occupy positions of trust and authority, thinking men and women of all classes, have their attention fixed upon the events taking place about us. They are watching the relations that exist among the nations. They observe the intensity that is taking possession of every earthly element, and they recognize that something great and decisive is about to take place—that the world is on the verge of a stupendous crisis.

"The Bible, and the Bible only, gives a correct view of these things. Here are revealed the great final scenes in the history of our world, events that already are casting their shadows before, the sound of their approach causing the earth to tremble and men's hearts to fail them for fear." P.K 535-537

6 The Generation Concept: Basic Principles

In our last chapter we studied the basic principles which drive the cyclical flow of history. In this chapter we shall apply these principles to the study of God's dealing with His people and their response to His grace. Always remember that...

> "The work of God in the earth presents, from age to age, a striking similarity in every great reformation or religious movement. The principles of God's dealing with men are ever the same. The important movements of the present have their parallel in those of the past, and the experience of the church in former ages has lessons of great value for our own time." GC 343

The Number 40

The **time period** required for the **maturation** of the **choice** and **direction** of any particular generation (post-Flood) is revealed in scripture to be 40 years, which equals one functional generation. Notice that we are not talking about a **biological** generation but about a **functional** generation. And the **function** is the **maturation** and **fixedness** of the choice of the people as a whole.

*"And your children shall wander in the wilderness forty years,
and bear your whoredoms, until your carcases be wasted
in the wilderness. After the number of the days in which
ye searched the land, even forty days, each day for a year,
shall ye bear your iniquities, even forty years, and ye shall
know my breach of promise." Numbers 14:33,34*

*"Wherefore as the Holy Ghost saith, To day if ye will hear
his voice, Harden not your hearts, as in the provocation, in
the day of temptation in the wilderness: When your fathers
tempted me, proved me, and saw my works forty years.
Wherefore I was grieved with that generation, and said,
They do alway err in their heart; and they have not known
my ways." Heb 3:7-10*

Before we go any further let us list for your personal study some
scriptural references which reveal the mysterious significance of
the number 40:

Forty days
Length of flood . . . . Gen 7:13
Jacob's embalming . . . . Gen 50:2,3
Moses on Mt. Sinai . . . . Ex 24:18
Spies in Canaan . . . . Num 13:25
Moses' prayer . . . . Deut 9:25-29
Goliath's arrogance . . . . 1 Sam 17:16
Elijah's fast . . . . 1 Ki 19:2,8
Nineveh's probation . . . . . . Jonah 3:4
Christ's temptation . . . . Luke 4:1,2
Christ's ministry after
his resurrection . . . . Acts 1:3

Forty stripes
Limit for scourging . . . . Deut 25:3
Paul's, one less . . . . 2 Cor 11:24

Forty years
Isaac's age at marriage . . . . Gen 25:20
Israel's diet . . . . Ex 16:35
Israel's wanderings . . . . Num 32:13
Same shoes for . . . . Deut 29:5
Period of rest . . . . Judg 3:11

Egypt's desolation........ Ezek 29:11-13
Saul's reign.............. Acts 13:21
David's reign .... 1 Ki 2:11
Solomon's reign .... 1 Ki 11:42

Returning now to the initial equation (40 years = 1 generation—maturation of choice), the prophet Joel, in Joel 1:1–4, explains that it takes 4 generations to make up **one** complete cycle of **sowing** and **reaping**. This is confirmed by God Himself in Exodus 20:5:

> *"...for I the LORD thy God am a jealous God, visiting the*
> *iniquity of the fathers upon the children unto the third and*
> *fourth generation of them that hate me;"*

4 generations = 1 cycle of sowing and reaping. We can therefore express these facts using the number code of Exodus 20:5:

Number of Generations			
1	2	3	4
Sown			Reaped

This number code is seen in the history of world empires after the Flood. The prophecies of Daniel predicted, and history has confirmed, that there would be only 4 world ruling empires. The iniquity sown in the first empire, **Babylon**, developed through the second, **Medo-Persia**, and the third, **Greece**, into complete collapse of imperial unity by the time the fourth, **Rome**, had ended.

History of Empires after the Flood — Daniel Chapters 2,7,8			
1 **Babylon**	**2** **Medo-Persia**	**3** **Greece**	**4** **Rome**
Seeds of			**Harvest of**
Iniquity,			**Disunity and**
Selfishness,			**Collapse of**
and Division			**World Empire**
Sown			**Reaped**

The prophet Daniel foretold that after the collapse of the Roman empire, any attempt to produce political unity in a world empire would be doomed to failure, read Daniel 2:40-43 and notice the finality of the disunity: *"... but they shall not cleave one to another ..."* Daniel 2:43

This number code is also seen in the history of Christianity from apostolic times to the times of the great Roman Catholic apostacy. From Revelation 2:

Number Codes in the History of Christianity			
1 ⇒	**2** ⇒	**3** ⇒	**4**
Ephesus	**Smyrna**	**Pergamos**	**Thyatira**
31–100A.D.	100–321A.D.	321–538A.D.	538–1600A.D.
Pure Church, but already the mystery of iniquity sown **2 Thes 2:7**	**Period of severe persecution** **Continued growth of mystery of iniquity** ⇒ ⇒ ⇒	**Period of compromise**	**Period of complete apostasy** **resulting in the Papacy, the "Falling away of"** **2 Thes 2:3**

The seeds of "the falling away" which were sown in the Ephesus period developed slowly at first because persecution kept the church pure. After Constantine's conversion and Sunday legislation (321 A.D.), the development of apostasy was stimulated by compromise until the full falling away was reaped in the apostasy of papal corruption which dominated Europe for more than a thousand years!

Since its development, the Papacy has remained and **will** remain a **permanently** false and apostate church, the mother of harlots of Revelation 17. Notice again the **finality** of the harvest of apostasy at the **fourth** level of succession.

Revelation chapter 6 parallels Revelation 2,3 but presents its symbolic pictures within the context of the review phase of the judgement. The book sealed with 7 seals represents the **information storage system** of heaven. (See C.O.L 294).

The opening of the first **four** seals pictures four horses which parallel the four successive periods from the Apostolic era to the Papal era. A colour code is now introduced by Revelation 6:

Color Codes in the History of Christianity						
	1	⇨	2	⇨	3	⇨	4
Rev 2	Ephesus		Smyrna		Pergamos		Thyatira
Rev 6	White		Red		Black		Pale
	Purity		Persecution		Compromise		Spritual death

So far we have established two equations in Bible mathematics:

1 generation = 40 years

1 cycle = 4 generations

In Matthew 23:32 the Bible speaks about a **"measure"**. Jesus told the Pharisees in His day that in their rejection of Him they would fill up the **"measure"** of their fathers.

"Fill ye up then the measure of your fathers." Matt 23:32

Back in Jeremiah 30:11 God had told His people, with regards to their Babylonian captivity, that He would correct them in **measure**. The Hebrew word for **"measure"** here is **"mishpat"** which means **Judgement**.

"For I am with thee, saith the LORD, to save thee: though I make a full end of all nations whither I have scattered thee, yet will I not make a full end of thee: but I will correct thee in measure, and will not leave thee altogether unpunished." Jer 30:11

There is another term used interchangeably with the term **measure;** that other term is **"cup."**

"For thus saith the LORD God of Israel unto me; Take the wine cup of this fury at my hand, and cause all the nations, to whom I send thee, to drink it. And they shall drink, and be moved, and be mad, because of the sword that I will send among them. Then took I the cup at the LORD'S hand, and made all the nations to drink, unto whom the LORD had sent me: To wit, Jerusalem, and the cities of Judah, and

the kings thereof, and the princes thereof, to make them a desolation, an astonishment, an hissing, and a curse; as it is this day;" Jeremiah 25:15-18

But how do we correlate a **cup** or **measure** with the two previous equations? Matthew 1:17 gives the answer:

"So all the generations from Abraham to David are fourteen generations; and from David until the carrying away into Babylon are fourteen generations; and from the carrying away into Babylon unto Christ are fourteen generations." Matt 1:17

Matthew 1:17 further elucidates the mysterious mathematical principles involved in the **time** analysis of the outworking of **cause** & **effect** events in the great controversy between light and darkness.

In the duration of time between the call of Abraham and the birth of Christ, the Israelites underwent **three** distinct periods of 14 generations each.

Between Abraham and David their general trend was upward, and, under David's rule the kingdom enjoyed such prosperity as was unknown to the Israelites before or after David. Under David, Israel reaped the reward of loyalty to God which was maintained by previous God-fearing leaders, (notwithstanding the apostasy of some, e.g. Saul).

After David, there was a downward trend of apostasy which resulted in Babylonian captivity.

It is noteworthy that Saul, David and Solomon each reigned for 40 years. In other words, each exerted his influence for an entire (functional) generation! Saul was Israel's **first** king, David was the **second** king, and Solomon the **third**. After Solomon, that is, **in the fourth** generation of monarchial government, the kingdom became divided. God through Samuel had warned them of the consequences of monarchial government. The judgmental reaping began to be more fully felt in the fourth generation after the first king, again confirming the principle of Exodus 20:5 *"visiting the iniquity of the fathers unto the third and fourth generation."*

After the Babylonian captivity, the Jews encased themselves in rigid legalistic orthodoxy and departed so far from God that in the fullness of time, Jesus had to come to show them the light. Daniel 8:23-25; Galatians 4:4,5.

Each 14 generation period produced a result representing a **measure** or a **cup** of **cause** → **effect** cycles. Therefore: 14 generations = one measure or cup (Matthew 1:17; Matthew 23:32). Jesus told the Jews in His day that their rejection of Him would fill up the **measure** of their fathers' iniquity.

1 cup or measure = 14 generations

At 3 cups or measures the fullness of time to redeem had come.

> *"But when the fulness of the time was come, God sent forth his Son, made of a woman, made under the law, To redeem them that were under the law, that we might receive the adoption of sons." Gal 4:4,5*

Let us now summarize the Biblical mathematics:

40 years = 1 generation (maturation of choice)

4 generations = 1 cycle of sowing and reaping

14 generations = 3 $^1/_2$ cycles = 1 measure or cup

Time Analysis Of The 2300 Year Prophecy

The earthly Old Testament sanctuary was rebuilt after Babylonian captivity. So too the truth of the Heavenly Sanctuary was restored after it had been trampled underfoot by the papacy (the mother of modern Babylon). Between 457 B.C. and 1844 A.D. were 2300 years or 57 $^1/_2$ generations = 14 complete cycles = 4 measures.

But 4 is the judgement number! Therefore after 4 measures the time of judgement had come. From 457 BC to 1844 AD = 2300 years = 4 measures. Therefore in 1844 Autumn the hour of God's Judgement had arrived!

Consider carefully the diagram on the following page:

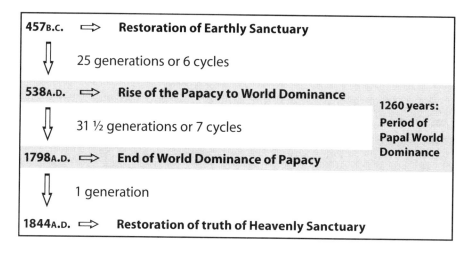

As 1844 approached, God initiated a wonderful work of revival in the earth through the proclamation of the First Angel's message within the context of the doctrine of the Second Coming of Christ. In the USA William Miller at first and others later on were called to present the message of the Second Coming of Christ and the prophecies of Daniel and the Revelation. Miller entered upon his work in 1831 and by 1840 the Advent Movement revival started to peak to a Spirit anointed intensity.

Miller and his associates misunderstood the event which was to occur at the end of the 2300 years of Daniel 8:14. They thought that Christ would return on October 22nd, 1844. But the prophecy foretold **not** the second coming of Christ to earth but the coming of Christ to the Most Holy Place in the Heavenly Sanctuary to commence the final phase of His High Priestly ministration.

Since 1844 Christ has been ministering and waiting for His remnant church to be harvest ripe and ready for His second coming.

But there has been a long delay! Why?

In our next chapter we shall apply the principles of the Generation Concept to Adventist history in order to get the answer.

7 The Application of the Generation Concept to Adventist History

Introduction

The **third angel's message** started to be proclaimed very soon after the great disappointment of October 22, 1844. Our High Priest, Jesus Christ, entered the Most Holy Place of the Heavenly Sanctuary on Oct 22, 1844 to commence the last phase of His High Priestly mediation for His people on earth. This last phase is called **"cleansing the sanctuary"** in Daniel 8:14 and it really means the total vindication of God's government through the perfecting of the character of His remnant end-time believers.

All who victoriously finish their Christian walk in Christ will have their sins blotted out and their names retained in the Book of Life.

> *"He that overcometh, the same shall be clothed in white raiment; and I will not blot out his name out of the book of life, but I will confess his name before my Father, and before his angels." Rev 3:5*

> *"Repent ye therefore, and be converted, that your sins may be blotted out, when the times of refreshing shall come from the presence of the Lord;" Acts 3:19*

And for the living remnant-elect, this work of blotting out their sins will occur while they are still alive. They will be made harvest-ripe and harvest-ready in Jesus Christ through the Holy Spirit by the third angel's message!

The third angel's message contains a number of beautiful truths, such as the correct interpretation of the prophecies of Daniel and Revelation in explaining the meaning of the **beast, its image** and **its mark,** and the order of last day events. It includes the previous two messages (Rev 14:6-12) and the basic doctrines of true Adventism.

But, most importantly, the third angel's message presents the full gospel of **righteousness by faith** and the **character of God,** thereby, and therefore, producing the end-time remnant who fully reflect the character of God and are harvest-ripe for the "sickle". The third angel's message concludes with a description of the harvest-ripe remnant in Rev 14:12:

> *"Here is the patience of the saints: here are they that*
> *keep the commandments of God, and the faith of Jesus."*
> *Rev 14:12*

It was Heaven's intention to bring the remnant to perfection within a relatively short period of time!

The First Generation.

The **first generation** in **the third angel's movement** was the **forty year** period 1844 to 1884. It was certainly God's intention to finish the work in that first generation (G1)! The Lord's servant, Sis Ellen White, certainly expected the Second Coming of Christ in that **first generation** after 1844. In fact, she expected the Lord's return **earlier** rather than **later** in that generation! In 1856 she wrote:

> "I was shown the company present at the Conference. Said the angel: "Some food for worms, some subjects of the seven last plagues, some will be alive and remain upon the earth to be translated at the coming of Jesus."
> 1T 131, 132 (1856). LDE 36

In 1872 she wrote:

> "Because time is short, we should work with diligence and double energy. Our children may never enter college."
> 3T 159 (1872)

And in 1876 she wrote:

> "In this age of the world, as the scenes of earth's history are soon to close and we are about to enter upon the time of trouble such as never was, the fewer the marriages contracted the better for all, both men and women." 5T 366 (1885).

> "The hour will come; it is not far distant, and some of us who now believe will be alive upon the earth, and shall see the prediction verified, and hear the voice of the archangel and the trump of God echo from mountain and plain and sea to the uttermost parts of the earth." RH July 31, 1888.

In 1883, as that first generation period drew to its close, Sister White wrote these words:

> "Had Adventists after the great disappointment in 1844 held fast their faith and followed on unitedly in the opening providence of God, receiving the message of the third angel and in the power of the Holy Spirit proclaiming it to the world, they would have seen the salvation of God, the Lord would have wrought mightily with their efforts, the work would have been completed, and Christ would have come ere this to receive His people to their reward. ...It was not the will of God that the coming of Christ should be thus delayed...For forty years did unbelief, murmuring, and rebellion shut out ancient Israel from the land of Canaan. The same sins have delayed the entrance of modern Israel into the heavenly Canaan. In neither case were the promises of God at fault. It is the unbelief, the worldliness, unconsecration, and strife among the Lord's professed people that have kept us in this world of sin and sorrow so many years." Ev 695, 696 (1883).

So we see clearly then, that God had intended to finish the work in that first generation and quite early too!

But there was a delay! Why?

The seeds of lukewarmness were sown early in that first generation. Writing in the 1850's the Servant of the Lord penned the following solemn warning.

> "Dear Brethren and Sisters: The Lord has shown me in
> vision some things concerning the church in its present
> lukewarm state, which I will relate to you. The church
> was presented before me in vision. Said the angel to the
> church: "Jesus speaks to thee, 'Be zealous and repent.'"
> This work, I saw, should be taken hold of in earnest. There
> is something to repent of. Worldly-mindedness, selfishness,
> and covetousness have been eating out the spirituality and
> life of God's people." 1T 141

The critical spiritual pathology in the Laodicean lukewarm
condition is an absence of the gospel as a vital, living experience.

The Lord sent warning upon warning to the church in that first
generation but it was in vain. Not that some individuals did not
respond but the church as a whole did not allow the messages
to prepare it for the harvest. Generation one (G1) ended and the
church was **not** harvest-ripe!

The Second Generation

The **second generation** in the third angel's movement of Seventh-
day Adventism was the period 1884 to 1924 (G2). At the start of
that generation, the time had arrived for God to pour out a special
blessing of grace, light and truth. Indeed it was time for the
proclamation of an acceptable year of the Lord.

To crown off all the warnings He had been sending throughout
the period of generation one, God sent a most precious message
early in the second generation.

It happened in 1888 at the Minneapolis General Conference
session in the autumn of that year.

> "The Lord in His great mercy sent a most precious message
> to His people through Elders Waggoner and Jones. This
> message was to bring more prominently before the world
> the uplifted Saviour, the sacrifice for the sins of the whole
> world. It presented justification through faith in the
> Surety; it invited the people to receive the righteousness
> of Christ, which is made manifest in obedience to all the
> commandments of God. Many had lost sight of Jesus. They
> needed to have their eyes directed to His divine person,

His merits, and His changeless love for the human family. All power is given into His hands, that He may dispense rich gifts unto men, imparting the priceless gift of His own righteousness to the helpless human agent. This is the message that God commanded to be given to the world. It is the third angel's message, which is to be proclaimed with a loud voice, and attended with the outpouring of His Spirit in a large measure." TM 91,92

What a declaration! And why was such a gracious message sent?

"The uplifted Saviour is to appear in His efficacious work as the Lamb slain, sitting upon the throne, to dispense the priceless covenant blessings, the benefits He died to purchase for every soul who should believe on Him. John could not express that love in words; it was too deep, too broad; he calls upon the human family to behold it. Christ is pleading for the church in the heavenly courts above, pleading for those for whom He paid the redemption price of His own lifeblood. Centuries, ages, can never diminish the efficacy of this atoning sacrifice. The message of the gospel of His grace was to be given to the church in clear and distinct lines, that the world should no longer say that Seventh-day Adventists talk the law, the law, but do not teach or believe Christ.

"The efficacy of the blood of Christ was to be presented to the people with freshness and power, that their faith might lay hold upon its merits. As the high priest sprinkled the warm blood upon the mercy seat, while the fragrant cloud of incense ascended before God, so while we confess our sins and plead the efficacy of Christ's atoning blood, our prayers are to ascend to heaven, fragrant with the merits of our Saviour's character. Notwithstanding our unworthiness, we are ever to bear in mind that there is One that can take away sin and save the sinner. Every sin acknowledged before God with a contrite heart, He will remove. This faith is the life of the church. As the serpent was lifted up in the wilderness by Moses, and all that had been bitten by the fiery serpents were bidden to look and live, so also the Son of man must be lifted up, that "whosoever believeth in Him should not perish, but have everlasting life."

"Unless he makes it his life business to behold the uplifted Saviour, and by faith to accept the merits which it is his privilege to claim, the sinner can no more be saved than Peter could walk upon the water unless he kept his eyes fixed steadily upon Jesus. Now, it has been Satan's determined purpose to eclipse the view of Jesus and lead men to look to man, and trust to man, and be educated to expect help from man. For years the church has been looking to man and expecting much from man, but not looking to Jesus, in whom our hopes of eternal life are centered. Therefore God gave to His servants a testimony that presented the truth as it is in Jesus, which is the third angel's message, in clear, distinct lines." TM 92,93

But alas! This gracious message was not allowed to do its God intended work. Of course there were individuals who accepted the message but the church in general and especially the leadership did not respond in the way that Heaven intended them to. And even though some of the leaders repented and confessed in the years that followed 1888, the messages did not produce a harvest-ripe remnant church in that second generation period.

The following solemn warning issued a few years after 1888 is worth penitent consideration even today.

Warning Against Despising God's Message

"I would speak in warning to those who have stood for years resisting light and cherishing the spirit of opposition. How long will you hate and despise the messengers of God's righteousness? God has given them His message. They bear the word of the Lord. There is salvation for you, but only through the merits of Jesus Christ. The grace of the Holy Spirit has been offered you again and again. Light and power from on high have been shed abundantly in the midst of you. Here was evidence, that all might discern whom the Lord recognized as His servants. But there are those who despised the men and the message they bore.

They have taunted them with being fanatics, extremists, and enthusiasts. Let me prophesy unto you: Unless you speedily humble your hearts before God, and confess your sins, which are many, you will, when it is too late, see that you have been fighting against God. Through the conviction of the Holy Spirit, no longer unto reformation and pardon, you will see that these men whom you have spoken against have been as signs in the world, as witnesses for God. Then you would give the whole world if you could redeem the past, and be just such zealous men, moved by the Spirit of God to lift your voice in solemn warning to the world; and, like them, to be in principle firm as a rock. Your turning things upside down is known of the Lord. Go on a little longer as you have gone, in rejection of the light from heaven, and you are lost. *'The man that shall be unclean, and shall not purify himself, that soul shall be cut off from among the congregation.'*

"I have no smooth message to bear to those who have been so long as false guideposts, pointing the wrong way. If you reject Christ's delegated messengers, you reject Christ. Neglect this great salvation, kept before you for years, despise this glorious offer of justification through the blood of Christ and sanctification through the cleansing power of the Holy Spirit, and there remaineth no more sacrifice for sins, but a certain fearful looking for of judgment and fiery indignation. I entreat you now to humble yourselves and cease your stubborn resistance of light and evidence. Say unto the Lord, Mine iniquities have separated between me and my God. O Lord, pardon my transgressions. Blot out my sins from the book of Thy remembrance. Praise His holy name, there is forgiveness with Him, and you can be converted, transformed.

"For if the blood of bulls and of goats, and the ashes of an heifer sprinkling the unclean, sanctifieth to the purifying of the flesh: how much more shall the blood of Christ, who through the eternal Spirit offered Himself without spot to God, purge your conscience from dead works to serve the living God?" TM 96,97,98

The 1888 message on the **covenants** and **righteousness by faith** presented the message to the Laodiceans of Revelation 3:14-22 within the context of the full, true, everlasting gospel. Heaven waited expectantly but to no avail!

There was abundant opportunity throughout that second generation period for repentance, revival and reformation. Writing in 1903 concerning what could have happened in the 1901 General Conference Session, Sis E.G. White penned these solemn words.

> "One day at noon I was writing of the work that might have been done at the last [1901] General Conference if the men in positions of trust had followed the will and way of God. Those who have had great light have not walked in the light. **The meeting was closed, and the break was not made. Men did not humble themselves before the Lord as they should have done, and the Holy Spirit was not imparted.**

> "I had written thus far when I lost consciousness, and I seemed to be witnessing a scene in Battle Creek.

> "We were assembled in the auditorium of the Tabernacle. Prayer was offered, a hymn was sung, and prayer was again offered. Most earnest supplication was made to God. The meeting was marked by the presence of the Holy Spirit. ...

> "No one seemed to be too proud to make heartfelt confession, and those who led in this work were the ones who had influence, but had not before had courage to confess their sins.

> "There was rejoicing such as never before had been heard in the Tabernacle. Then I aroused from my unconsciousness, and for a while could not think where I was. My pen was still in my hand. The words were spoken to me: 'This might have been. **All this the Lord was waiting to do for His people. All heaven was waiting to be gracious." I thought of where we might have been had thorough work been done at the last General Conference.'"**
> 8T 104-106 (Jan. 5, 1903). LDE 57-58

After that warning the second generation period passed on routinely. The servant of the Lord, Sis E.G. White, died in 1915.

Great changes started to develop in the world (e.g. the first world war, Atheistic Communism). The Advent message continued to spread and develop globally but Generation Two ended and the harvest was not ripe! The 1888 message according to the Hosea prophecy would have to wait for a future day for acceptance.

> *"I will go and return to my place, till they acknowledge their offence, and seek my face: in their affliction they will seek me early. Come, and let us return unto the LORD: for he hath torn, and he will heal us; he hath smitten, and he will bind us up. After two days will he revive us: in the third day he will raise us up, and we shall live in his sight. Then shall we know, if we follow on to know the LORD: his going forth is prepared as the morning; and he shall come unto us as the rain, as the latter and former rain unto the earth."* Hosea 5:15; 6:1-3

The Third Generation

According to the principle of sowing and reaping in Exodus 20:5, the iniquity of the **fathers** is visited upon the **third** and **fourth** generations.

The seeds of lukewarmness sown in the first generation, coupled with the fact that there was no ripening response to the 1888-1901 messages of the covenants, righteousness by faith and advanced gospel order in the second generation, meant that the third and fourth generations would reap the disastrous consequences of generation one (G1) iniquity!

The **third** generation in Adventism was the period 1924 to 1964. During the 1950's there occurred the meetings with Drs Barnhouse and Martin which led to compromise and apostasy on the human nature of Christ in the incarnation and confusing terminology on the **final atonement** in the Heavenly sanctuary.

There was no way generation three (G3) could have been ready for the harvest when profound and widespread ignorance of the heaven-sent 1888 message existed throughout the length and breadth of Adventism.

But in the 1950's there was also a rediscovery of the Jones-Waggoner messages which, vis-a-vis the compromises of that same decade, led to increasing agitation and honest enquiry in the Adventist world.

The Fourth Generation

The fourth generation of Adventism was 1964-2004. What a generation the fourth has been! It has seen tremendous events both in Adventism and the world at large! Two distinct sets of developments occurred in generation four (G4).

One set of events has to do with the on-going principle of Exodus 20:5. The effects of G1 iniquity have been severely felt in G4.

The other set of events has to do with the on-going principle of Hosea 6:1-3. The fourth generation (G4) was the **third day** of the Hosea 6:2 principle and God has been reestablishing the true seventh day Adventism through the wonderful truths of the Jones-Waggoner messages on the covenants and righteousness by faith.

There has therefore been progressive "shaking" in the Adventist world. Ever since 1964 more and more individual Adventists have been exposed to the Jones-Waggoner messages and many have accepted the wonderful light. Some of them have continued to walk in the advancing light of God's glory according to Hosea 6:1-3.

The glorious messages of the righteousness of Christ and the Character of our God are doing a great work of preparing a people who are following on to know the Lord.

This is evidence enough that we are now in the third day of Hosea 6:1-3 and we are moving on to the final latter rain baptismal outpouring of the Holy Spirit.

At the same time doctrinal confusion persists in Laodicean Adventism. As a result of rejecting the true doctrine of the covenants and human nature of Christ Jesus, the truths of Christian character perfection and final atonement in the Most Holy Place are being rejected by many.

In the world at large, we have witnessed some startling events in the *fourth* generation since 1844. Here is a comprehensive list (by no means complete):

a) The sudden fall of Communism in the 1989 to 1992 period, thus setting free Eastern Europe for religious outreach and for the final reality of Papal European unification.

b)   The fall of apartheid in South Africa, thereby setting free another sector of humanity.

c)   The rapid rise of the Papacy to world popularity.

d)   Increasing world problems of all kinds, e.g. the H.I.V. epidemic, economic instability, lawlessness, crime, environmental pollution and corruption, terrorism, drug trafficking.

e)   The increasing call for Sunday sacredness.

f)   The continued and rapid development of spiritism and its disguised infiltration into the evangelical churches.

g)   The now unchallenged supremacy of the U.S.A., its announced role of establishing and sustaining a New World Economic Order and its fight against global terrorism.

Conclusion

The harvest was not ripened in either the first or second generation of Adventism, even though Heaven made special efforts to achieve a harvest-ripe remnant.

The third and fourth generations were therefore left to reap the consequences of the earlier iniquity. Four generations have been completed since 1844.

> "The angels of God in their messages to men represent time as very short. Thus it has always been presented to me. It is true that time has continued longer than we expected in the early days of this message. Our Saviour did not appear as soon as we hoped. But has the Word of the Lord failed? Never! It should be remembered that the promises and threatenings of God are alike conditional…We may have to remain here in this world because of insubordination many more years, as did the children of Israel, but for Christ's sake His people should not add sin to sin by charging God with the consequence of their own wrong course of action.
> Ev 695, 696 (1901). LDE 38, 39

8 Important Lessons From Generation One

Be Zealous and Repent—E.G.White: Testimonies Vol. 1

"Dear Brethren and Sisters: The Lord has shown me in vision some things concerning the church in its present lukewarm state, which I will relate to you. The church was presented before me in vision. Said the angel to the church: *'Jesus speaks to thee, "Be zealous and repent."'* This work, I saw, should be taken hold of in earnest. There is something to repent of. Worldly-mindedness, selfishness, and covetousness have been eating out the spirituality and life of God's people.

"The danger of God's people for a few years past has been the love of the world. Out of this have sprung the sins of selfishness and covetousness. The more they get of this world, the more they set their affections on it; and still they reach out for more. Said the angel: *'It is easier for a camel to go through a needle's eye, than for a rich man to enter into the kingdom of God.'* Yet many who profess to believe that we are having the last note of warning to the world, are striving with all their energies to place themselves in a position where it is easier for a camel to go through a needle's eye than for them to enter the kingdom.

"These earthly treasures are blessings when rightly used. Those who have them should realize that they are lent them of God and should cheerfully spend their means to advance His cause. They will not lose their reward here. They will be kindly regarded by the angels of God and will also lay up a treasure in heaven.

"I saw that Satan watches the peculiar, selfish, covetous temperament of some who profess the truth, and he will tempt them by throwing prosperity in their path, offering them the riches of earth. He knows that if they do not overcome their natural temperament, they will stumble and fall by loving mammon, worshiping their idol. Satan's object is often accomplished. The strong love of the world overcomes, or swallows up, the love of the truth. The kingdoms of the world are offered them, and they eagerly grasp their treasure and think they are wonderfully prospered. Satan triumphs because his plan has succeeded. They have given up the love of God for the love of the world.

"I saw that those who are thus prospered can thwart the design of Satan if they will overcome their selfish covetousness by laying all their possessions upon the altar of God. And when they see where means are needed to advance the cause of truth and to help the widow, the fatherless, and afflicted, they should give cheerfully and thus lay up treasure in heaven.

"Heed the counsel of the True Witness. Buy gold tried in the fire, that thou mayest be rich, white raiment that thou mayest be clothed, and eyesalve that thou mayest see. Make some effort. These precious treasures will not drop upon us without some exertion on our part. We must buy—"be zealous and repent" of our lukewarm state. We must be awake to see our wrongs, to search for our sins, and to zealously repent of them.

"I saw that the brethren who have possessions have a work to do to tear away from these earthly treasures and to overcome their love of the world. Many of them love this world, love their treasure, but are not willing to see it. They must be zealous and repent of their selfish covetousness, that the love of the truth may swallow up everything else. I saw that many of those who have riches will fail to buy the gold, white raiment, and eyesalve. Their zeal does not possess intensity and earnestness proportionate to the value of the object of which they are in pursuit.

"I saw these men while striving for the possessions of earth; what zeal they manifested, what earnestness, what energy to obtain an earthly treasure that must soon pass away! What cool calculations they made! They plan and toil early and late, and sacrifice their ease and comfort for earthly treasure. A corresponding zeal on their part to obtain the gold, white raiment, and eyesalve will bring them in possession of these desirable treasures and life, everlasting life, in the kingdom of God. I saw that if any need eyesalve, it is those who have earthly possessions. Many of them are blind to their own state, blind to their firm grasp upon this world. Oh, that they may see!

"*'Behold, I stand at the door, and knock: if any man hear My voice, and open the door, I will come in to him, and will sup with him, and he with Me.'* I saw that many have so much rubbish piled up at the door of their heart that they cannot get the door open. Some have difficulties between themselves and their brethren to remove. Others have evil tempers, selfish covetousness, to remove before they can open the door. Others have rolled the world before the door of their heart, which bars the door. All this rubbish must be taken away, and then they can open the door and welcome the Saviour in.

"Oh, how precious was this promise, as it was shown to me in vision! "I will come in to him, and will sup with him, and he with Me." Oh, the love, the wondrous love of God! After all our lukewarmness and sins He says: "Return unto Me, and I will return unto thee, and will heal all thy backslidings." This was repeated by the angel a number of times. "Return unto Me, and I will return unto thee, and will heal all thy backslidings."

"Some, I saw, would gladly return. Others will not let this message to the Laodicean church have its weight upon them. They will glide along, much after the same manner as before, and will be spewed out of the mouth of the Lord. Those only who zealously repent will have favor with God.

"To him that overcometh will I grant to sit with Me in My throne, even as I also overcame, and am set down with My Father in His throne." We can overcome. Yes; fully, entirely. Jesus died to make a way of escape for us, that we might overcome every evil temper, every sin, every temptation, and sit down at last with Him.

"It is our privilege to have faith and salvation. The power of God has not decreased. His power, I saw, would be just as freely bestowed now as formerly. It is the church of God that have lost their faith to claim, their energy to wrestle, as did Jacob, crying: "I will not let Thee go, except Thou bless me." Enduring faith has been dying away. It must be revived in the hearts of God's people. There must be a claiming of the blessing of God. Faith, living faith, always bears upward to God and glory; unbelief, downward to darkness and death.

"I saw that the minds of some of the church have not run in the right channel. There have been some peculiar temperaments that have had their notions by which to measure their brethren. And if any did not exactly agree with them, there was trouble in the camp at once. Some have strained at a gnat and swallowed a camel.

"These set notions have been humored and indulged altogether too long. There has been a picking at straws. And when there were no real difficulties in the church, trials have been manufactured. The minds of the church and the servants of the Lord are called from God, truth, and heaven to dwell upon darkness. Satan delights to have such things go on; it feasts him. But these are none of the trials which are to purify the church and that will in the end increase the strength of God's people.

"I saw that some are withering spiritually. They have lived some time watching to keep their brethren straight—watching for every fault to make trouble with them. And while doing this, their minds are not on God, nor on heaven, nor on the truth; but just where Satan wants them—on someone else. Their souls are neglected; they seldom see or feel their own faults, for they have had enough to do to watch the faults of others without so much as looking to their own souls or searching their own hearts. A person's dress, bonnet, or apron takes their attention. They must talk to this one or that one, and it is sufficient to dwell upon for weeks. I saw that all the religion a few poor souls have consists in watching the garments and acts of others, and finding fault with them. Unless they reform, there will be no place in heaven for them, for they would find fault with the Lord Himself.

"Said the angel: *'It is an individual work to be right with God.'* The work is between God and our own souls. But when persons have so much care of others' faults, they take no care of themselves. These notional, faultfinding ones would often cure themselves of the habit if they would go directly to the individual they think is wrong. It would be so crossing that they would give up their notions rather than go. But it is easy to let the tongue run freely about this one or that one when the accused is not present.

"Some think it is wrong to try to observe order in the worship of God. But I have seen that it is not dangerous to observe order in the church of God. I have seen that confusion is displeasing to the Lord, and that there should be order in praying and also in singing. We should not come to the house of God to pray for our families unless deep feeling shall lead us while the Spirit of God is convicting them. Generally, the proper place to pray for our families is at the family altar. When the subjects of our prayers are at a distance, the closet is the proper place to plead with God for them. When in the house of God, we should pray for a present blessing and should expect God to hear and answer our prayers. Such meetings will be lively and interesting.

"I saw that all should sing with the spirit and with the understanding also. God is not pleased with jargon and discord. Right is always more pleasing to Him than wrong. And the nearer the people of God can approach to correct, harmonious singing, the more is He glorified, the church benefited, and unbelievers favorably affected.

"I have been shown the order, the perfect order, of heaven, and have been enraptured as I listened to the perfect music there. After coming out of vision, the singing here has sounded very harsh and discordant. I have seen companies of angels, who stood in a hollow square, everyone having a harp of gold. At the end of the harp was an instrument to turn to set the harp or change the tunes. Their fingers did not sweep over the strings carelessly, but they touched different strings to produce different sounds. There is one angel who always leads, who first touches the harp and strikes the note, then all join in the rich, perfect music of heaven. It cannot be described. It is melody, heavenly, divine, while from every countenance beams the image of Jesus, shining with glory unspeakable." 1T 141-146

The Laodicean Church

"God leads His people on, step by step. He brings them up to different points calculated to manifest what is in the heart. Some endure at one point, but fall off at the next. At every advanced point the heart is tested and tried a little closer. If the professed people of God find their hearts opposed to this straight work, it should convince them that they have a work to do to overcome, if they would not be spewed out of the mouth of the Lord. Said the angel: *'God will bring His work closer and closer to test and prove every one of His people.'* Some are willing to receive one point; but when God brings them to another testing point, they shrink from it and stand back, because they find that it strikes directly at some cherished idol. Here they have opportunity to see what is in their hearts that shuts out Jesus. They prize something higher than the truth, and their hearts are not prepared to receive Jesus. Individuals are tested and proved a length of time to see if they will sacrifice their idols and heed the counsel of the True Witness. If any will not be purified through obeying the truth, and overcome their selfishness, their pride, and evil passions, the angels of God have the charge: *'They are joined to their idols, let them alone,'* and they pass on to their work, leaving these with their sinful traits unsubdued, to the control of evil angels. Those who come up to every point, and stand every test, and overcome, be the price what it may, have heeded the counsel of the True Witness, and they will receive the latter rain, and thus be fitted for translation.

"God proves His people in this world. This is the fitting-up place to appear in His presence. Here, in this world, in these last days, persons will show what power affects their hearts and controls their actions. If it is the power of divine truth, it will lead to good works. It will elevate the receiver, and make him noblehearted and generous, like his divine Lord. But if evil angels control the heart, it will be seen in various ways. The fruit will be selfishness, covetousness, pride, and evil passions.

"The heart is deceitful above all things, and desperately wicked. Professors of religion are not willing to closely examine themselves to see whether they are in the faith; and it is a fearful fact that many are leaning on a false hope. Some lean upon an old experience which they had years ago; but when brought down to this heart-searching time, when all should have a daily experience, they have nothing to relate. They seem to think that a profession of the truth will save them. When they subdue those sins which God hates, Jesus will come in and sup with them and they with Him. They will then draw divine strength from Jesus, and will grow up in Him, and be able with holy triumph to say: "Thanks be to God, which giveth us the victory through our Lord Jesus Christ." It would be more pleasing to the Lord if lukewarm professors of religion had never named His name. They are a continual weight to those who would be faithful followers of Jesus. They are a stumbling block to unbelievers, and evil angels exult over them, and taunt the angels of God with their crooked course. Such are a curse to the cause at home or abroad. They draw nigh to God with their lips, while their heart is far from Him.

"I was shown that the people of God should not imitate the fashions of the world. Some have done this, and are fast losing the peculiar, holy character which should distinguish them as God's people. I was pointed back to God's ancient people, and was led to compare their apparel with the mode of dress in these last days. What a difference! what a change! Then the women were not so bold as now. When they went in public, they covered their faces with a veil. In these last days, fashions are shameful and immodest. They are noticed in prophecy. They were first brought in by a class over whom Satan has entire control, who, *'being past feeling* [without any conviction of the Spirit of God] *have given themselves over unto lasciviousness, to work all uncleanness with greediness.'* If God's professed people had not greatly departed from Him, there would now be a marked difference between their dress and that of the world. The small bonnets, exposing the face and head, show a lack of modesty. The hoops are a shame. The inhabitants of earth are growing more and more corrupt, and the line of distinction between them and the Israel of God must be more plain, or the curse which falls upon worldlings will fall on God's professed people.

"I was directed to the following scriptures. Said the angel: *'They are to instruct God's people.'* 1 Timothy 2:9, 10: *'In like manner also, that women adorn themselves in modest apparel, with shamefacedness and sobriety; not with broided hair, or gold, or pearls, or costly array; but (which becometh women professing Godliness) with good works.'*"1 Peter 3:3-5: *'Whose adorning let it not be that outward adorning of plaiting the hair, and of wearing of gold, or of putting on of apparel; but let it be the hidden man of the heart, in that which is not corruptible, even the ornament of a meek and quiet spirit, which is in the sight of God of great price. For after this manner in the old time the holy women also, who trusted in God, adorned themselves.'*

"Young and old, God is now testing you. You are deciding your own eternal destiny. Your pride, your love to follow the fashions of the world, your vain and empty conversation, your selfishness, are all put in the scale, and the weight of evil is fearfully against you. You are poor, and miserable, and blind, and naked. While evil is increasing and taking deep root, it is choking the good seed which has been sown in the heart; and soon the word that was given concerning Eli's house will be spoken to the angels of God concerning you: Your sins *'shall not be purged with sacrifice nor offering forever.'* Many, I saw, were flattering themselves that they were good Christians, who have not a single ray of light from Jesus. They know not what it is to be renewed by the grace of God. They have no living experience for themselves in the things of God. And I saw that the Lord was whetting His sword in heaven to cut them down. Oh, that every lukewarm professor could realize the clean work that God is about to make among His professed people! Dear friends, do not deceive yourselves concerning your condition. You cannot deceive God. Says the True Witness: *'I know thy works.'* The third angel is leading up a people, step by step, higher and higher. At every step they will be tested.

"The plan of systematic benevolence is pleasing to God. I was pointed back to the days of the apostles, and saw that God laid the plan by the descent of His Holy Spirit, and that by the gift of prophecy He counseled His people in regard to a system of benevolence. All were to share in this work of imparting of their carnal things to those who ministered unto them in spiritual things. They were also taught that the widows and fatherless had a claim upon their charity. Pure and undefiled religion is defined, To visit the widows and fatherless in their affliction, and to keep unspotted from the world. I saw that this was not merely to sympathize with them by comforting words in their affliction, but to aid them, if needy, with our substance. Young men and women to whom God has given health can obtain a great blessing by aiding the widow and the fatherless in their affliction. I saw that God requires young men to sacrifice more for the good of others. He claims more of them than they are willing to perform. If they keep themselves unspotted from the world, cease to follow its fashions, and lay by that which the lovers of pleasure spend in useless articles to gratify pride, and give it to the worthy afflicted ones, and to sustain the cause, they will have the approval of Him who says, "I know thy works."

"There is order in heaven, and God is well pleased with the efforts of His people in trying to move with system and order in His work on earth. I saw that there should be order in the church of God, and that system is needed in carrying forward successfully the last great message of mercy to the world. God is leading His people in the plan of systematic benevolence, and this is one of the very points to which God is bringing up His people which will cut the closest with some. With them this cuts off the right arm, and plucks out the right eye, while to others it is a great relief. To noble, generous souls the demands upon them seem very small, and they cannot be content to do so little. Some have large possessions, and if they lay by them in store for charitable purposes as God has prospered them, the offering seems to them like a large sum. The selfish heart clings as closely to a small offering as to a larger one, and makes a small sum look very large.

"I was pointed back to the commencement of this last work. Then some who loved the truth could consistently talk of sacrificing. They devoted much to the cause of God, to send the truth to others. They have sent their treasure beforehand to heaven. Brethren, you who have received the truth at a later period, and who have large possessions, God has called you into the field, not merely that you may enjoy the truth, but that you may aid with your substance in carrying forward this great work. And if you have an interest in this work, you will venture out and invest something in it, that others may be saved by your efforts, and you reap with them the final reward. Great sacrifices have been made and privations endured to place the truth in a clear light before you. Now God calls upon you, in your turn, to make great efforts and to sacrifice in order to place the truth before those who are in darkness. God requires this. You profess to believe the truth; let your works testify to the fact. Unless your faith works, it is dead. Nothing but a living faith will save you in the fearful scenes which are just before you.

"I saw that it is time for those who have large possessions to begin to work fast. It is time that they were not only laying by them in store as God is now prospering them, but as He has prospered them. In the days of the apostles, plans were especially laid that some should not be eased and others burdened. Arrangements were made that all should share equally in the burdens of the church of God according to their several abilities. Said the angel: *'The ax must be laid at the root of the tree.'* Those who, like Judas, have set their hearts upon earthly treasure will complain as he did. His heart coveted the costly ointment poured upon Jesus, and he sought to hide his selfishness under a pious, conscientious regard for the poor: *'Why was not this ointment sold for three hundred pence, and given to the poor?'* He wished that he had the ointment in his possession; it would not thus be lavished upon the Saviour. He would apply it to his own use; sell it for money. He prized his Lord just enough to sell Him to wicked men for a few pieces of silver. As Judas brought up the poor as an excuse for his selfishness, so professed Christians, whose hearts are covetous, will seek to hide their selfishness under a put-on conscientiousness. Oh, they fear that in adopting systematic benevolence we are becoming like the nominal churches! *'Let not thy left hand know what thy right hand doeth.'* They seem to have a conscientious desire to follow exactly the Bible as they understand it in this matter; but they entirely neglect the plain admonition of Christ: *'Sell that ye have, and give alms.'*

"*'Take heed that ye do not your alms before men, to be seen of them.'* Some think this text teaches that they must be secret in their works of charity. And they do but very little, excusing themselves because they do not know just how to give. But Jesus explained it to His disciples as follows: *'Therefore when thou doest thine alms, do not sound a trumpet before thee, as the hypocrites do in the synagogues and in the streets, that they may have glory of men. Verily I say unto you, they have their reward.'* They gave to be regarded noble and generous by men. They received praise of men, and Jesus taught His disciples that this was all the reward they would have. With many, the left hand does not know what the right hand does, for the right hand does nothing worthy of the notice of the left hand. This lesson of Jesus to His disciples was to rebuke those who wished to receive glory of men. They performed their almsgiving at some very public gathering; and before doing this, a public proclamation was made heralding their generosity before the people; and many gave large sums merely to have their name exalted by men. And the means given in this manner was often extorted from others, by oppressing the hireling in his wages, and grinding the face of the poor.

"I was shown that this scripture does not apply to those who have the cause of God at heart, and use their means humbly to advance it. I was directed to these texts: *'Let your light so shine before men, that they may see your good works, and glorify your Father which is in heaven.'* *'By their fruits ye shall know them.'* I was shown that Scripture testimony will harmonize when it is rightly understood. The good works of the children of God are the most effectual preaching that the unbeliever has. He thinks that there must be strong motives that actuate the Christian to deny self, and use his possessions in trying to save his fellow men. It is unlike the spirit of the world. Such fruits testify that the possessors are genuine Christians. They seem to be constantly reaching upward to a treasure that is imperishable.

"With every gift and offering there should be a suitable object before the giver, not to uphold any in idleness, not to be seen of men or to get a great name, but to glorify God by advancing His cause. Some make large donations to the cause of God while their brother who is poor, may be suffering close by them, and they do nothing to relieve him. Little acts of kindness performed for their brother in a secret manner would bind their hearts together, and would be noticed in heaven. I saw that in their prices and wages the rich should make a difference in favor of the afflicted and widows and the worthy poor among them. But it is too often the case that the rich take advantage of the poor, reaping every benefit that is to be gained, and exacting the last penny for every favor. It is all written in heaven. *'I know thy works.'*

"The greatest sin which now exists in the church is covetousness. God frowns upon His professed people for their selfishness. His servants have sacrificed their time and strength to carry them the word of life, and many have shown by their works that they prize it but lightly. If they can help the servant of God just as well as not, they sometimes do it; but they often let him pass on, and do but little for him. If they employ a day laborer, he must be paid full wages. But not so with the self-sacrificing servant of God. He labors for them in word and doctrine; he carries the heavy burden of the work on his soul; he patiently shows from the word of God the dangerous errors which are hurtful to the soul; he enforces the necessity of immediately tearing up the weeds which choke the good seed sown; he brings out of the storehouse of God's word things new and old to feed the flock of God. All acknowledge that they have been benefited; but the poisonous weed, covetousness, is so deeply rooted that they let the servant of God leave them without ministering to him of their temporal things. They have prized his wearing labor just as highly as their acts show. Says the True Witness: *'I know thy works.'*

"I saw that God's servants are not placed beyond the temptations of Satan. They are often fearfully beset by the enemy, and have a hard battle to fight. If they could be released from their commission, they would gladly labor with their hands. Their labor is called for by their brethren; but when they see it so lightly prized, they are depressed. True, they look to the final settlement for their reward, and this bears them up; but their families must have food and clothing. Their time belongs to the church of God;

it is not at their own disposal. They sacrifice the society of their families to benefit others; and yet some who are benefited by their labors are indifferent to their wants. I saw that it is doing injustice to such to let them pass on and deceive themselves. They think they are approved of God, when He despises their selfishness. Not only will these selfish ones be called to render an account to God for the use they have made of their Lord's money, but all the depression and heartache which they have brought upon God's chosen servants, and which have crippled their efforts, will be set to the account of the unfaithful stewards.

"The True Witness declares: *'I know thy works.'* The selfish, covetous heart will be tested. Some are not willing to devote to God a very small portion of the increase of their earthly treasure. They would start back with horror if you should speak of the principal. What have they sacrificed for God? Nothing. They profess to believe that Jesus is coming; but their works deny their faith. Every person will live out all the faith he has. False-hearted professor, Jesus knows thy works. He hates your stinted offerings, your lame sacrifices." 1T 185-195

9 To Proclaim the Acceptable Year of the LORD

A Word Study of "To Proclaim the Acceptable Year of the Lord"

The Word "Year"

The Hebrew word translated **"year"** in Isaiah 61:2 is the word *shanah* which literally means **"a repetition."** The other Hebrew word usually translated **year** is *yamin* which literally means **days** (e.g.) 1 Kings 1:1). It is very important to know that the word used in Isaiah 61:2 is **shanah** which does not mean **year** in the ordinary sense of the term but rather means a **repetition**, a **cycle**!

Similarly in the Greek there are several words translated **"year."** Here are some examples:

ETOS (a year) Luke 2:36

HEMERAI (days) Luke 1:7

DIETES (2 years) Matthew 2:16

However, the word used in Luke 4:19 is the word *eniautos* which like the Hebrew word *shanah* means a **repetition**, a **revolution; a cycle**!

The Word "Acceptance"

The Hebrew word is ***ratson*** which means "**good pleasure**".

The Word to "Proclaim"

The Hebrew word is ***qara*** which means "**to call**" or "**to declare**".

The Entire Statement

The Hebrew words translated "**to proclaim the acceptable year of the Lord**" are "**qara ratson shanah YAHWEH**". The Greek interlinear Diaglott translates Luke 4:19 as follows: "**To proclaim an era of acceptance with the Lord**".

The term "**qara ratson shana Yahweh**" really means "to announce that the time of God's good pleasure has come around again!" In other words, as history has flowed in cycles, in revolution, in repetitions, the time has come around again for Jesus to call it the time or era for YAHWEH'S good pleasure.

The History Of The Term

"To proclaim the acceptable era of YAHWEH" is a Messianic term. In Old Testament typology there were several occasions when God visited His people with special favour and deliverance. One immediately recalls the Exodus of Israel from Egypt under Moses and the deliverance of the captives from Babylonian captivity and their return to Jerusalem to rebuild the temple and city under Ezra and Nehemiah. Both the **Exodus** and the **Return of the Exiles** were **types** of the glorious Messianic redemptive deliverance accomplished by our Saviour, Jesus Christ, at the cross in His first advent and, of course, the final triumphant "exodus" of all the people of God from this world into the kingdom of glory at Christ's Second Coming! The Apostle Paul has left a beautiful summary of the first advent redemptive deliverance in Colossians Chapter 1. Let us read a few pertinent verses:

> "*Giving thanks unto the Father, which hath made us meet to be partakers of the inheritance of the saints in light: Who hath delivered us from the power of darkness, and hath*

translated us into the kingdom of his dear Son: In whom we have redemption through his blood, even the forgiveness of sins:" Col. 1:12-14

"And, having made peace through the blood of his cross, by him to reconcile all things unto himself; by him, I say, whether they be things in earth, or things in heaven. And you, that were sometime alienated and enemies in your mind by wicked works, yet now hath he reconciled in the body of his flesh through death, to present you holy and unblameable and unreproveable in his sight: If ye continue in the faith grounded and settled, and be not moved away from the hope of the gospel, which ye have heard, and which was preached to every creature which is under heaven; whereof I Paul am made a minister;" Col 1:20-23

Paul also looked forward to the final deliverance in Hebrews 9:28:

"So Christ was once offered to bear the sins of many; and unto them that look for him shall he appear the second time without sin unto salvation." Hebrews 9:28

The Specific Historical Basis Found In Leviticus

The Lord had given to Israel a beautiful socio-economic system based upon the number 7 and built upon the truth of genuine Sabbath rest and deliverance. That system is described in Leviticus chapter 25. A.T. Jones referred to it as the gospel in Leviticus. Before we go any further let us open our Bibles and read Leviticus 25.

The basic principle is found in Exodus 23:10-12

"And six years thou shalt sow thy land, and shalt gather in the fruits thereof: But the seventh year thou shalt let it rest and lie still; that the poor of thy people may eat: and what they leave the beasts of the field shall eat. In like manner thou shalt deal with thy vineyard, and with thy olive yard. Six days thou shalt do thy work, and on the seventh day thou shalt rest: that thine ox and thine ass may rest, and the son of thy handmaid, and the stranger, may be refreshed." Exodus 23:10-12

We can now write down some divine mathematical principles:

6 Days Of Work **+** The 7th Day Sabbath	**=** 1 Week Of Days	
6 Years Of Agriculture **+** 7th Year Of Rest	**=** 1 Week Of Years For The Land	
7 Sabbaths Or Weeks Of Years 7x7=49 Years	The 50th Year Was Jubilee	

We can go further:

6 Millenia **+** The 7th Millenium **=** 1 Week Of Millenia		
6 Years Of History The Millenium of Rev 20 7000 Years from Gen 1 to Rev 21:11		

The Lord's servant commenting on these divine principles wrote as follows in *Review And Herald* September 17, 1889.

> "Every seventh year, special provision was made for the poor. The sabbatical year, as it was called, began at the end of the harvest. At the seed-time, which followed the ingathering, the people were not to sow. They should not dress the vineyard in the spring, and they must expect neither harvest nor vintage. Of that which the land produced spontaneously, they might eat while fresh, but they were not to lay up any portion of it in their storehouses. The yield of this year was to be free for the stranger, the fatherless, and the widow, and even for the creatures of the field.

> "But if the land ordinarily produced only enough to supply the wants of the people, how were they to subsist during the year when no crops were gathered? For this the promise of God made ample provision. *'I will command my blessing upon you in the sixth year,'* he said, *'and it shall bring forth fruit for three years. And ye shall sow the eighth year, and eat yet of old fruit until the ninth year; until her fruits come in ye shall eat of the old store.'*

> "The observance of the sabbatical year was to be a benefit to both the land and the people. The soil, lying untilled for one season, would afterward produce more plentifully. The people were released from the pressing labors of the field; and while there were various branches of work that could be followed during this time, all enjoyed greater leisure, which

afforded opportunity for the restoration of their physical powers for the exertions of the following years. They had more time for meditation and prayer, for acquainting themselves with the teachings and requirements of the Lord, and for the instruction of their households.

"In the sabbatical year the Hebrew slaves were to be set at liberty, and they were not to be sent away portionless. The Lord's direction was, "When thou sendest him out free from thee, thou shalt not let him go away empty. Thou shalt furnish him liberally out of thy flock, and out of thy floor, and out of thy wine-press. Of that wherewith the Lord thy God hath blessed thee thou shalt give unto him."

"The hire of the laborer was to be promptly paid: "Thou shalt not oppress a hired servant that is poor and needy, whether he be of thy brethren, or of thy strangers that are in thy land. . . . At his day thou shalt give him his hire, neither shall the sun go down upon it; for he is poor, and setteth his heart upon it."

"Special directions were also given concerning the treatment of fugitives from service: "Thou shalt not deliver unto his master the servant which is escaped from his master unto thee. He shall dwell with thee, even among you, in that place which he shall choose in one of thy gates, where it liketh him best; thou shalt not oppress him."

"To the poor, the seventh year was a year of release from debt. The Hebrews were enjoined at all times to assist their needy brethren by lending them money without interest. To take usury from a poor man was expressly forbidden: "If thy brother be waxen poor, and fallen in decay with thee, then thou shalt relieve him; yea, though he be a stranger, or a sojourner; that he may live with thee. Take thou no usury of him, or increase: but fear thy God; that thy brother may live with thee. Thou shalt not give him thy money upon usury, nor lend him thy victuals for increase." If the debt remained unpaid until the year of release, the principal itself could not be recovered. The people were expressly warned against withholding from their brethren needed assistance on account of this: "If there be among you a poor man of one of thy brethren, . . . thou shalt not harden thine heart, nor shut thine hand from thy poor brother...Beware that there be not a thought in thy wicked heart, saying, The seventh year, the year of release, is at hand; and thine eye be evil against thy poor brother, and thou givest him naught; and he cry unto the Lord against thee, and it be sin unto thee." "The poor shall never cease out of the land; therefore I command thee, saying, Thou shalt open thine hand wide unto thy brother, to thy poor, and to thy needy, in thy land," "and shalt surely lend him sufficient for his need, in that which he wanteth."

"None need fear that their liberality would bring them to poverty. Obedience to God's commandments would surely result in prosperity. "Thou shalt lend unto many nations," he said, "but thou shalt not borrow; and thou shalt reign over many nations, but they shall not reign over thee."

"After seven "sabbaths of years," "seven times seven years," came the great year of release,—the jubilee. "Then shalt thou cause the trumpet of the jubilee to sound . . . throughout all your land. And ye shall hallow the fiftieth year, and proclaim liberty throughout all the land unto all the inhabitants thereof; it shall be a jubilee unto you; and ye shall return every man unto his possession, and ye shall return every man unto his family."

""On the tenth day of the seventh month, in the day of atonement," the trumpet of the jubilee was sounded. Throughout the land, wherever the Jewish people dwelt, the sound was heard, calling upon all the children of Jacob to welcome the year of release. On the great Day of Atonement, satisfaction was made for the sins of Israel, and with gladness of heart the people would welcome the jubilee.

"As in the sabbatical year, the land was not to be sown nor reaped, and all that it produced was to be regarded as the rightful property of the poor. Certain classes of Hebrew slaves–all who did not receive their liberty in the sabbatical year – were now set free.

"But that which especially distinguished the year of jubilee was the reversion of all landed property to the family of the original possessor. By the special direction of God, the land had been divided by lot. After the division was made, no one was at liberty to trade his estate. Neither was he to sell his land unless poverty compelled him to do so, and then, whenever he or any of his kindred might desire to redeem it, the purchaser must not refuse to sell it; and if unredeemed, it would revert to its first possessor or his heirs in the year of jubilee. RH Sept 17, 1889

The Acceptable Year Of Our Lord Contains The Jubilee Principle

The central principle in the Jubilee was and is **redemptive deliverance**:

"That which especially distinguished the year of jubilee was the reversion of all land property to the family of the original possessor." RH Sept 17, 1889.

Therefore when Jesus stood up that Sabbath and declared that He was anointed by His Father to preach the good news to the poor, to heal the brokenhearted, to preach deliverance to the captives, and recovering of sight to the blind, to liberate the oppressed and preach the acceptable era of YAHWEH, He was in fact declaring that He had come to **buy back** or **redeem all** that had been sold out! Hallejujah! He had come to remove the condemnation to eternal death that had fallen upon Adam's lost race. He had come to reconcile fallen humanity to God! He was proclaiming the Jubilee of full and free forgiveness of all sins as well as deliverance from the bondage to sin!

The Ultimate Jubilee

When God delivers His living remnant-elect in the great time of trouble from destruction by the mark-of-the-beast authorities, the final Jubilee will begin!

"And at that time shall Michael stand up, the great prince which standeth for the children of thy people: and there shall be a time of trouble, such as never was since there

was a nation even to that same time: and at that time thy people shall be delivered, every one that shall be found written in the book." Daniel 12:1

"And the seventh angel poured out his vial into the air; and there came a great voice out of the temple of heaven, from the throne, saying, It is done." Rev 16:17

"It was at midnight that God chose to deliver His people. As the wicked were mocking around them, suddenly the sun appeared, shining in His strength, and the moon stood still. The wicked looked upon the scene with amazement, while the saints beheld with solemn joy the tokens of their deliverance. Signs and wonders followed in quick succession. Everything seemed turned out of its natural course. The streams ceased to flow. Dark, heavy clouds came up and clashed against each other. But there was one clear place of settled glory, whence came the voice of God like many waters, shaking the heavens and the earth. There was a mighty earthquake. The graves were opened, and those who had died in faith under the third angel's message, keeping the Sabbath, came forth from their dusty beds, glorified, to hear the covenant of peace that God was to make with those who had kept His law.

"The sky opened and shut and was in commotion. The mountains shook like a reed in the wind and cast out ragged rocks all around. The sea boiled like a pot and cast out stones upon the land. And as God spoke the day and the hour of Jesus' coming and delivered the everlasting covenant to His people, He spoke one sentence, and then paused, while the words were rolling through the earth. The Israel of God stood with their eyes fixed upward, listening to the words as they came from the mouth of Jehovah and rolled through the earth like peals of loudest thunder. It was awfully solemn. At the end of every sentence the saints shouted, "Glory! Hallelujah!" Their countenances were lighted up with the glory of God, and they shone with glory as did the face of Moses when he came down from Sinai. The wicked could not look upon them for the glory.

And when the never-ending blessing was pronounced on those who had honored God in keeping His Sabbath holy, there was a mighty shout of victory over the beast and over his image.

"**Then commenced the jubilee**, when the land should rest. I saw the pious slave rise in victory and triumph, and shake off the chains that bound him, while his wicked master was in confusion and knew not what to do; for the wicked could not understand the words of the voice of God.

"Soon appeared the great white cloud, upon which sat the Son of man. When it first appeared in the distance, this cloud looked very small. The angel said that it was the sign of the Son of man. As it drew nearer the earth, we could behold the excellent glory and majesty of Jesus as He rode forth to conquer. A retinue of holy angels, with bright, glittering crowns upon their heads, escorted Him on His way. No language can describe the glory of the scene. The living cloud of majesty and unsurpassed glory came still nearer, and we could clearly behold the lovely person of Jesus. He did not wear a crown of thorns, but a crown of glory rested upon His holy brow. Upon His vesture and thigh was a name written, King of kings, and Lord of lords. His countenance was as bright as the noonday sun, His eyes were as a flame of fire, and His feet had the appearance of fine brass. His voice sounded like many musical instruments. The earth trembled before Him, the heavens departed as a scroll when it is rolled together, and every mountain and island were moved out of their places.
"And the kings of the earth, and the great men, and the rich men, and the chief captains, and the mighty men, and every bondman, and every freeman, hid themselves in the dens and in the rocks of the mountains; and said to the mountains and rocks, Fall on us, and hide us from the face of Him that sitteth on the throne, and from the wrath of the Lamb: for the great day of His wrath is come; and who shall be able to stand?" Those who a short time before would have destroyed God's faithful children from the earth, now witnessed the glory of God which rested upon them. And

amid all their terror they heard the voices of the saints in joyful strains, saying, "Lo, this is our God; we have waited for Him, and He will save us."

"The earth mightily shook as the voice of the Son of God called forth the sleeping saints. They responded to the call and came forth clothed with glorious immortality, crying, "Victory, victory, over death and the grave! O death, where is thy sting? O grave, where is thy victory?" Then the living saints and the risen ones raised their voices in a long, transporting shout of victory. Those bodies that had gone down into the grave bearing the marks of disease and death came up in immortal health and vigor. The living saints are changed in a moment, in the twinkling of an eye, and caught up with the risen ones, and together they meet their Lord in the air. Oh, what a glorious meeting! Friends whom death had separated were united, never more to part.

"On each side of the cloudy chariot were wings, and beneath it were living wheels; and as the chariot rolled upward, the wheels cried, "Holy," and the wings, as they moved, cried, "Holy," and the retinue of holy angels around the cloud cried, "Holy, holy, holy, Lord God Almighty!" And the saints in the cloud cried, "Glory! Alleluia!" And the chariot rolled upward to the Holy City. Before entering the city, the saints were arranged in a perfect square, with Jesus in the midst. He stood head and shoulders above the saints and above the angels. His majestic form and lovely countenance could be seen by all in the square." EW 285,286

Modern-Day Application to Adventist History

The 2300 year prophecy ended in autumn 1844. The believers who had gone through the Great Disappointment had a wonderful opportunity, **indeed an acceptable era,** for becoming harvest-ripe for the Second Coming. They missed their opportunity and that acceptable era was in vain!

Lukewarmness became the endemic spiritual malady of Adventism and it was severe and chronic by the end of that first generation in 1844.

But God in His great mercy and love sent another special time of opportunity, another acceptable era, in 1888. He sent the remedy for Laodicean lukewarmness in the Jones-Waggoner message of the covenants and righteousness by faith. That message started in 1888, 4 years after the end of the first generation. And had the message been allowed to do its heaven intended work, the final events would have been ushered in quite rapidly, in other words, the Jubilee could have occurred very early in the second generation.

We have already seen, that even at the 1901 General Conference session all heaven had been waiting to be gracious. In other words, that was also another acceptable era which was missed!

Well, the third generation saw deepening confusion and apostasy but in 1950 a wonderful opportunity was again presented to the Church leadership in the Wieland and Short appeal to penitently accept the Jones-Waggoner light. That opportunity was also missed.

Our time Now

We have passed the end of the fourth generation and we are into the "fifth" generation. But in biblical generational mathematics it must be correctly called the **first** generation of a **new** cycle because the fourth generation ends a cycle.

> *"But in the fourth generation they shall come hither again: for the iniquity of the Amorites is not yet full." Genesis 15:16*

> *"Thou shalt not bow down thyself to them, nor serve them: for I the LORD thy God am a jealous God, visiting the iniquity of the fathers upon the children unto the third and fourth generation of them that hate me;" Exodus 20:5*

According to the Hosea 5:15; 6:1-3 principle the message of righteousness by faith visited in Generation 2. That was its first day of visitation and it was rejected (Hosea 5:15). After "two days" would have to mean in the **fourth** generation. Throughout the fourth generation 1964-2004 there has been increasingly progressive dissemination of the Jones-Waggoner messages on the covenants and righteousness by faith along with the advancing light on the character of God and glorification. Hosea 6:3 declares:

> *"Then shall we know, if we follow on to know the LORD: his going forth is prepared as the morning; and he shall come unto us as the rain, as the latter and former rain unto the earth." Hosea 6:3*

This means that out of the shaking of the fourth generation will emerge those who will follow on to know the Lord and receive the "latter rain" baptism of power. And if we have learnt well the lessons of the past, there is no reason why we should not let the Lord *"finish the work and cut it short in righteousness"* (Romans 9:28) **very early** in the **new** first generation.

10 Nearest of Kin
by **A.T. Jones**

"Who was the redeemer in the book of Ruth? The nearest of kin. Boaz could not come in as redeemer until it was found that the one who was nearer than he could not perform the office of redeemer. The redeemer must be not only one who was near of kin, but he must be the nearest among those who were near, and therefore Boaz could not step into the place of redeemer until, by another's stepping out of the place, he became really the nearest. Now that is the precise point that is made in the second chapter of Hebrews.

"In Ruth, you remember Naomi's husband had died, the inheritance had fallen into the hands of others, and when she came back from Moab, it had to be redeemed. No one but the nearest of kin could do it. This is the story also in the second of Hebrews. Here is the man Adam, who had an inheritance—the earth—and he lost it and he himself was brought into bondage. In the gospel in Leviticus it is preached that if one had lost his inheritance, himself and his inheritance could be redeemed, but only the nearest of kin could redeem. Lev. 25:25, 26, 47-49. Upon earth here is a man, Adam, who lost his inheritance and himself, and you and I were in it all, and we need a redeemer. But only he who is nearest in blood relationship can perform the office of redeemer. Jesus Christ is nearer than a brother, nearer than anyone. He is a brother, but He is nearest among the brethren, nearest of kin, actually. Not only one with us but He is one of us and one with us by being one of us.

"And the one lesson that we are studying still and the leading thought is how entirely Jesus is ourselves. We found in the preceding lesson that He is altogether ourselves. In all points of temptation, wherever we are tempted, He was ourselves right there; in all the points in which it is possible for me to be tempted, He, as I, stood right there, against all the knowledge and ingenuity of Satan to tempt me, Jesus, myself, stood right there and met it. Against all the power of Satan put forth in the temptation upon me, Jesus stood as myself and overcame. So also with you and so with the other man, and thus comprehending the whole human race, He stands in every point wherever anyone of the human race can be tempted as in himself or from himself.

"In all this, He is ourselves and in Him we are complete against the power of temptation. In Him we are overcomers, because He, as we, overcame. 'Be of good cheer; I have overcome the world.' (John 16:33)

"And in noticing the other evening how he became one of us, we found that it was by birth from the flesh. He is 'the seed of David according to the flesh.' He took not the nature of angels but the nature of the seed of Abraham, and His genealogy goes to Adam.

"Now every man is tempted, you know, 'when he is drawn away of His own lust and enticed.' James 1:14. That is the definition of 'temptation.' There is not a single drawing toward sin, there is not a single tendency to sin, in you and me that was not in Adam when he stepped out of the garden. All the iniquity and all the sin that have come into the world came from that, and came from him as he was there. It did not all appear in him; it did not all manifest itself in him in open action, but it has manifested itself in open action in those who have come from him.

"Thus all the tendencies to sin that have appeared or that are in me came to me from Adam, and all that are in you came from Adam, and all that are in the other man came from Adam. So all the tendencies to sin that are in the human race came from Adam. But Jesus Christ felt these temptations; He was tempted upon all these points in the flesh which he derived from David, from Abraham, and from Adam. In his genealogy are a number of characters set forth as they were lived in the men, and they were not righteous. Manasseh is there, who did worse than any other king ever in Judah and caused Judah to do worse than the heathen. Solomon is there with the description of his character in the Bible just as it is. David is there. Rahab is there. Judah is there. Jacob is there. All are there just as they were. Now Jesus came according to the flesh at the end of that line of mankind. And there is such a thing as heredity. You and I have traits of character or cut of feature that have come to us from away back—perhaps not from our own father, perhaps not from a grandfather, but from a great-grandfather away back in the years. And this is referred to in the law of God: 'Visiting the iniquity of the fathers upon the children unto the third and fourth generation of them that hate me; and showing mercy unto thousands of them that love me and keep my commandments.'

"That 'like produces like' is a good law, a righteous law. It is a law of God, and though the law be transgressed, it still does the same. Transgression of the law does not change the law, whether it be moral or physical. The law works when it is transgressed, through the evil that is incurred, just as it would have worked in righteousness always if no evil had ever been incurred. If man had remained righteous always, as God made him, his descent would have been in the right line. When the law was transgressed, the descent followed on the wrong line, and the law worked in the crooked way, by its being perverted.

"It is a good law which says that everything shall have a tendency to go toward the center of the earth. We could not get along in the world without that law. It is that which holds us upon the earth and enables us to walk and move about upon it. And yet if there be a break between us and the earth, if our feet slip out from under us or if we be on a high station, a pinnacle, and it breaks and the straight connection with the earth is broken between us and it, why, the law works and it brings us down with a terrible jolt, you know. Well, the same law that enables us to live and move and walk around upon the earth as comfortably as we do, which works so beneficially while we act in harmony with it, that law continues to work when we get out of harmony with it and it works as directly as before—but it hurts.

"Now that is simply an illustration of this law of human nature. If man had remained where God put him and as He put him, the law would have worked directly and easily; since man has got out of harmony with it, it still works directly, but it hurts. Now that law of heredity reached from Adam to the flesh of Jesus Christ as certainly as it reaches from Adam to the flesh of any of the rest of us, for He was one of us. In Him there were things that reached Him from Adam; in Him there were things that reached Him from David, from Manasseh, from the genealogy away back from the beginning until His birth.

"Thus in the flesh of Jesus Christ—not in Himself, but in His flesh—our flesh which He took in the human nature—there were just the same tendencies to sin that are in you and me. And when He was tempted, it was the 'drawing away of these desires that were in the flesh.' These tendencies to sin that were in His flesh drew upon Him and sought to entice Him, to consent to the wrong. But by the love of God and by His trust in God, he received the power and the strength and the grace to say, 'No,' to all of it and put it all under foot. And thus being in the likeness of sinful flesh He condemned sin in the flesh.

"All the tendencies to sin that are in me were in Him, and not one of them was ever allowed to appear in Him. All the tendencies to sin that are in you were in Him, and not one of them was ever allowed to appear—every one was put under foot and kept there. All the tendencies to sin that are in the other man were in Him, and not one of them was ever allowed to appear. That is simply saying that all the tendencies to sin that are in human flesh were in His human flesh, and not one of them was ever allowed to appear; He conquered them all. And in Him we all have victory over them all.

"Many of these tendencies to sin that are in us have appeared in action, and have become sins committed, have become sins in the open. There is a difference between a tendency to sin and the open appearing of that sin in the actions. There are tendencies to sin in us that have not yet appeared, but multitudes have appeared. Now all the tendencies that have not appeared, He conquered. What of the sins that have actually appeared? 'The Lord hath laid on Him the iniquity of us all' (Isa. 53:6) 'Who his own self bare our sins in his own body on the tree.' 1 Peter 2:24. Thus it is plain that all the tendencies to sin that are in us and have not appeared and all the sins which have appeared were laid upon Him. It is terrible. It is true. But, O, joy! In that terrible truth lies the completeness of our salvation.

"Note another view: Those sins which we have committed, we our-selves felt the guilt of them and were conscious of condemnation because of them. These were all imputed to Him. They were all laid upon Him. Now a question: Did He feel the guilt of the sins that were imputed to Him? Was He conscious of the condemnation of the sins — our sins — that were laid upon Him? He never was con-scious of sins that He committed, for He did not commit any. That is true. But our sins were laid upon Him and we were guilty. Did He realize the guilt of these sins? Was He conscious of condemnation because of these sins?

"We will look at that in such a way that every soul in the house shall say, 'Yes.' I will say that another way: We will look at it in such a way that every soul in the house will either say 'Yes' or may say 'Yes' if he will, because there may be some in the house who have not had the experience that I will bring for the illustration, but many have it, and then they can say, 'Yes.' All others who have had the experience will say 'Yes' at once.

"God imputes righteousness, the righteousness of Christ, unto the believing sinner. Here is a man who has never known anything in his life but sin, never anything but the guilt of sin, never anything but the condemnation of sin. That man believes on Jesus Christ, and God imputes to that man the righteousness of Christ. Then that man who never committed a particle of righteousness in his life is conscious of righteousness. Something has entered his life that was never there before. He is conscious of it, and he is conscious of the joy of it and the freedom of it.

"Now God imputed our sins to Jesus Christ as certainly as He imputes His righteousness to us. But when he imputes righteousness to us who are nothing but sinners, we realize it and are conscious of it and conscious of the joy of it. Therefore, when He imputed our sins to

Jesus, He was conscious of the guilt of them and the condemnation of them, just as certainly as the believing sinner is conscious of the righteousness of Christ and the peace and joy of it that is imputed to him — that is, that is laid upon him.

"In all this also, Jesus was precisely ourselves. Or in all points He was truly made like unto us. In all points of temptation He was ourselves. He was one of us in the flesh; He was ourselves, and thus He was ourselves in temptation. And in points in guilt and condemnation He was precisely ourselves, because it was our sins, our guilt and our condemnation that were laid upon Him.

"Now another thing upon what we have said: 'our sins' — how many of them? All were laid upon Him, and He carried the guilt and the condemnation of them all, and also answered for them, paid for them, atoned for them. Then in Him we are free from every sin that we have ever committed. That is the truth. Let us be glad of it and praise God with everlasting joy.

"He took all the sins which we have committed; He answered for them and took them away from us forever and all the tendencies to sin which have not appeared in actual sins — these he put forever under foot. Thus He sweeps the whole board and we are free and complete in Him.

"O, He is a complete Saviour. He is a Saviour from sins committed and the Conqueror of the tendencies to commit sins. In Him we have the victory. We are no more responsible for these tendencies being in us than we are responsible for the sun shining, but every man on earth is responsible for these things appearing in open action in Him, because Jesus Christ has made provision against their ever appearing in open action. Before we learned of Christ, many of them had appeared in open action. The Lord hath laid upon Him all these and He has taken them away. Since we learned of Christ, these tendencies which have not appeared He condemned as sin in the flesh. And shall He who believes in Jesus allow that which Christ condemned in the flesh to rule over Him in the flesh? This is the victory that belongs to the believer in Jesus.

"It is true that, although a man may have all this in Jesus, He cannot profit by it without himself being a believer in Jesus. Take the man who does not believe in Jesus at all tonight. Has not Christ made all the provision for him that He has for Elijah, who is in heaven tonight? And if this man wants to have Christ for his Saviour, if he wants provision made for all his sins and salvation from all of them, does Christ have to do anything now in order to provide for this man's sins or to save him from them? No. That is all done. He made all that provision for every man when He was in the flesh and every man who believes in Him receives this without there being any need of any part of it being done over again. He 'made one sacrifice for sins forever.' And having by Himself purged us from our sins, He sat down on the right hand of the Majesty on high. Thus it is all in Him and every believer in Him possesses it all in Him and in Him is complete. It is in Him and that is the blessedness of it. 'In Him dwelleth all the fullness of the godhead bodily.' And God gives His eternal Spirit and us eternal life — eternity in which to live — in order that that eternal Spirit may reveal to us and make known to us the eternal depths of the salvation that we have in Him whose goings forth have been from the days of eternity.

"Now let us look at it in another way. Turn to Romans 5:12:

"'Wherefore, as by one man sin entered into the world, and death by sin; and so death passed upon all men, for that all have sinned.'

"Now, leaving out the verses in parenthesis for the moment and reading them afterward, read the eighteenth verse:

"'Therefore, as by the offense of one [that man that sinned] judgment came upon all men to condemnation; even so by the righteousness of one [that Man that did not sin] the free gift came upon all men unto justification of life. For as by one man's disobedience [that man that sinned] many were made sinners, so by the obedience of one [that Man that did not sin] shall many be made righteous.'

"Now read the parenthesis:

"'For until the law sin was in the world: but sin is not imputed when there is no law. Nevertheless death reigned from Adam to Moses, even over them that had not sinned after the similitude of Adam's transgression, who is the figure of him that was to come.'

"Adam, then, was the figure of Him that was to come. That one to come is Christ. Adam was the figure of Him. Wherein was Adam the figure of Him? In his righteousness? No. For he did not keep it. In his sin? No. For Christ did not sin. Wherein, then, was Adam the figure of Christ? In this: That all that were in the world were included in Adam, and all that are in the world are included in Christ. In other words: Adam in his sin reached all the world; Jesus Christ, the second Adam, in His righteousness touches all humanity. That is where Adam is the figure of Him that was to come. So read on:

"'But not as the offense, so also is the free gift: for if through the offense of one many be dead, much more the grace of God and the gift by grace, which is by one man, Jesus Christ, hath abounded unto many.'

"There are two men, then, whom we are studying: That one man by whom sin entered; that one man by whom righteousness entered.

"'And not as it was by one that sinned, so is the gift: for the judgment was by one to condemnation but the free gift is of many offenses unto justification. For if by one man's offense death reigned by one [that is, by the first Adam]; much more they which receive abundance of grace and of the gift of righteousness shall reign in life by one, Jesus Christ [the second Adam].'

"Read another text in connection with this before we touch the particular study of it. 1 Cor. 15:45—49:

"'So it is written, The first man Adam was made a living soul; the last Adam was made a quickening spirit. Howbeit that was not first which is spiritual, but that which is natural; and afterward that which is spiritual. The first man is of the earth, earthy: the second man is the Lord from heaven. As is the earthy, such are they also that are earthy: and as is the heavenly, such are they also that are heavenly. And as we have borne the image of the earthy, we shall also bear the image of the heavenly.'

"The first Adam touched all of us; what he did included all of us. If he had remained true to God, that would have included all of us. And when he fell away from God, that included us and took us also. Whatever he should have done embraced us, and what he did made us what we are.

"Now here is another Adam. Does He touch as many as the first Adam did? That is the question. That is what we are studying now. Does the second Adam touch as many as did the first Adam? And the answer is that it is certainly true that what the second Adam did embraces all that were embraced in what the first Adam did. What he should have done, what he could have done, would embrace all.

"Suppose Christ had yielded to temptation and had sinned. Would that have meant anything to us? It would have meant everything to us. The first Adam's sin meant all this to us; sin on the part of the second Adam would have meant all this to us. The first Adam's righteousness would have meant all to us and the second Adam's righteousness means all to as many as believe. **That is correct in a certain sense, but not in the sense in which we are studying it now. We are now studying from the side of the Adams.** We will look at it from our side presently.

"The question is, Does the second Adam's righteousness embrace as many as does the first Adam's sin? Look closely. Without our consent at all, without our having anything to do with it, we were all included in the first Adam; we were there. All the human race were in the first Adam. What that first Adam—what that first man, did meant us; it involved us. That which the first Adam did brought us into sin, and the end of sin is death, and that touches every one of us and involves every one of us.

"Jesus Christ, the second man, took our sinful nature. He touched us 'in all points.' He became we and died the death. And so in Him, and by that, every man that has ever lived upon the earth and was involved in the first Adam is involved in this and will live again. There will be a resurrection of the dead, both of the just and of the unjust. Every soul shall live again by the second Adam from the death that came by the first Adam.

"'Well,' says one, 'we are involved in other sins besides that one.' Not without our choice. When God said, 'I will put enmity between thee and the woman and between thy seed and her seed,' He set every man free to choose which master he would serve, and since that, every man that has sinned in this world has done it because he chose to. 'If our gospel be hid, it is hid to them that are lost: in whom the god of this world hath blinded the minds of them which believe not.'—not them who had no chance to believe; the god of this world blinds no man until he has shut his eyes of faith. When he shuts his eyes of faith, then Satan will see that they are kept shut as long as possible. I read the text again: 'If our gospel,'—the everlasting gospel, the gospel of Jesus Christ which is Christ in you the hope of glory, from the days of the first Adam's sin until now—'if our gospel be hid, it is hid to them that are lost.' It is hid to them 'in whom the god of this world hath blinded the minds.' And why did he blind the minds? Because they 'believe not.' 2 Cor 4:3, 4.

"Abraham, a heathen, born a heathen, as all the rest of us are, and raised a heathen, grew up in a family of heathens, worshiping idols and the heavenly hosts. He turned from it all unto God and opened his eyes of faith and used them, and Satan never had a chance to blind his eyes. And Abraham, a heathen, thus turning from among heathens unto God and finding God in Jesus Christ in the fullness of hope—that is one reason why God has set him before all the world. He is an example of what every heathen on this earth may find. He is a God-set-forth example of how every heathen is without excuse if he does not find God in Jesus Christ, by the everlasting gospel. Abraham is set before all nations in witness of the fact that every heathen is responsible in his own way if he does not find what Abraham found.

"Therefore, just as far as the first Adam reaches man, so far the second Adam reaches man. The first Adam brought man under the condemnation of sin, even unto death; the second Adam's righteousness undoes that and makes every man live again. As soon as Adam sinned, God gave him a second chance and set him free to choose which master he would have. Since that time every man is free to choose which way he will go; therefore he is responsible for his own individual sins. And when Jesus Christ has set us all free from the sin and the death which came upon us from the first Adam, that freedom is for every man, and every man can have it for the choosing.

"The Lord will not compel any one to take it. He compels no one to sin and He compels no one to be righteous. Everyone sins upon his own choice. The Scriptures demonstrate it. And every one can be made perfectly righteous at his choice. And the Scriptures demonstrate this. No man will die the second death who has not chosen sin rather than righteousness, death rather than life. In Jesus Christ there is furnished in completeness all that man needs or ever can have in righteousness, and all there is for any man to do is to choose Christ and then it is his.

"So then as the first Adam was We, the second Adam is We. In all points He is as weak as are we. Read two texts: He says of us, 'Without me ye can do nothing.' Of Himself He says: 'Of mine own self I can do nothing.' (John 15:5, 5:30)

"These two texts are all we want now. They tell the whole story. To be without Christ is to be without God, and there the man can do nothing. He is utterly helpless of himself and in himself. That is where the man is who is without God. Jesus Christ says: 'Of mine own self I can do nothing.' Then that shows that the Lord Jesus put Himself in this world, in the flesh, in His human nature, precisely where the man is in this world who is without God. He put Himself precisely where lost man is. He left out His divine self and became we. **And there, helpless as we are without God, He ran the risk of getting back to where God is and bringing us with him. It was a fearful risk, but, glory to God, He won. The thing was accomplished, and in Him we are saved.**

"When He stood where we are, He said, 'I will put my trust in Him' and that trust was never disappointed. In response to that trust the Father dwelt in Him and with Him and kept Him from sinning. John 14:10. Who was He? We. And thus the Lord Jesus has brought to every man in this world divine faith. That is the faith of the Lord Jesus. That is saving faith. **Faith is not something that comes from ourselves with which we believe upon Him, but it is that something with which He believed—the faith which He exercised, which He brings to us, and which becomes ours and works in us—the gift of God. That is what the word means, 'Here are they that keep the commandments of God and the faith of Jesus.' They keep the faith of Jesus because it is that divine faith which Jesus exercised Himself.**

"He being we brought to us that divine faith which saves the soul—that divine faith by which we can say with Him, 'I will put my trust in Him.' And in so putting our trust in Him, that trust today will never be disappointed anymore than it was then. God responded then to the trust and dwelt with Him. God will respond today to that trust in us and will dwell with us.

"God dwelt with Him and He was ourselves. Therefore His name is Emmanuel, God with us. Not God with Him. God was with Him before the world was; He could have remained there and not come here at all and still God could have remained with Him and His name could have been God with Him. He could have come into this world as He was in heaven and His name could still have been God with Him. But that never could have been God with us. But what we needed was God with us. God with Him does not help us, unless He is we. But that is the blessedness of it. He who was one of God became one of us; He who was God became we, in order that God with Him should be God with us. O, that is His name! That is His name! Rejoice in that name forevermore—God with us!"

11 The Battle in the Mind
by **A.T. Jones**

"Now as to Christ's not having 'like passions' with us: In the Scriptures all the way through He is like us and with us according to the flesh. He is the seed of David according to the flesh. He was made in the likeness of sinful flesh. Don't go too far. He was made in the likeness of sinful flesh, not in the likeness of sinful mind. Do not drag His mind into it. His flesh was our flesh, but the mind was 'the mind of Christ Jesus.' Therefore it is written: 'Let this mind be in you which was also in Christ Jesus.' If He had taken our mind, how, then, could we ever have been exhorted to 'let this mind be in you which was also in Christ Jesus?' It would have been so already. But what kind of mind is ours? O, it is corrupted with sin also. Look at ourselves in the second chapter of Ephesians, beginning with the first verse and reading to the third, but the third verse is the one that has this particular point in it:

"'Among whom also we all had our conversation in times past in the lusts of our flesh, fulfilling the desires of the flesh and of the mind; and were by nature the children of wrath, even as others.' Eph 2:3

"Now I refer you also to page 191 of the Bulletin, to the lessons we studied on the destruction of that enmity. We studied there where the enmity came from, you remember—how it got into this world—the ground is covered in this that I have just read. Adam had the mind of Jesus Christ in the garden; he had the divine mind—the divine and the human were united, sinlessly. Satan came in and offered his inducements through the appetite, through the flesh. Adam and Eve forsook the mind of Jesus Christ, the mind of God that was in them, and accepted the suggestions and the leadings of this other mind. Thus they were enslaved to that and so are we all. Now Jesus Christ comes into the world, taking our flesh, and in His sufferings and temptations in the wilderness He fights the battle upon the point of appetite.

"Where Adam and Eve failed and where sin entered He fought the battle over and victory was won and righteousness entered. He having fasted forty days and forty nights—perfectly helpless, human as ourselves, hungry as we—there came to Him the temptation, 'If thou be the Son of God, command that these stones be made bread.' He answered, 'It is written, Man shall not live by bread alone, but by every word that proceedeth out of the mouth of God.'

"Then Satan took another turn. He argued: You are trusting in the word of God, are you? All right. Here the word of God says: 'He shall give his angels charge concerning thee: and in their hands they shall bear thee up, lest at any time thou dash thy foot against a stone.' Now you are trusting in the word of God: you jump off here, for it is written, 'He shall give his angels charge concerning thee.' Jesus answered again: 'It is written again, Thou shalt not tempt the Lord thy God.'

"Then Satan took Jesus upon an exceeding high mountain and showed Him all the glory of them too—the glory, the honor, the dignity—he showed Him all that. And there at that moment there was stirred up all the ambition that ever appeared in Napoleon or Caesar or Alexander or all of them put together. But from Jesus still the answer is: 'It is written, Thou shalt worship the Lord thy God, and him only shalt thou serve.'

"Then the devil departed from Him for a season, and angels came and ministered unto Him. There was the power of Satan conquered in man on the point of appetite—just where that power was gained over man. This man at the first had the mind of God; he forsook it and took the mind of Satan. In Jesus Christ the mind of God is brought back once more to the sons of men, and Satan is conquered. Therefore, it is gloriously true, as the word reads in Dr. Young's translation and in the German, as it does in the Greek: 'We know that the Son of God is come and has given us a mind.' 1 John 5:20

"Read the last words of 1 Cor. 2:16: 'We have the mind of Christ.' Put the two transactions together. The German and the Danish and also the Greek are alike. Put the two together: 'We know that the Son of God is come and has given us a mind' and 'We have the mind of Christ.' Thank the Lord!

"Read in Romans now. I will read from the Greek, beginning with the twenty-fourth verse of the seventh chapter. You remember from the tenth to the twenty-fourth verses is that contest: The good I would do, I do not; and the evil I hate, that I do. I find then a law, that, when I would do good, evil is present with me. I see another law in my members, warring against the law of my mind and bringing me into captivity to the law of sin which is in my members. There the flesh has control and draws the mind after it, fulfilling the desires of the flesh and of the mind. Now, Verse 24 and on into Romans 8.

"O wretched man that I am! Who shall deliver me from the body of this death? I thank God through Jesus Christ our Lord. So then I myself with the mind indeed serve the law of God [or rather serve God's law, literally here]; but with the flesh, sin's law. There is then now no condemnation to those in Christ Jesus who walk not according to flesh but according to Spirit. For the law of the Spirit of life in Christ Jesus set me free from the law of sin and of death. For the law being powerless, in that it was weak through the flesh, God having sent his own son in likeness of flesh of sin, and for sin, condemned sin in the flesh, that the requirement of the law should be fulfilled in us, who not according to flesh walk, but according to Spirit. For they that according to flesh are, the things of the flesh mind; and they according to Spirit, the things of the Spirit. For the mind of the flesh is death; but the mind of the Spirit [that is, the Spirit's mind; the one is the flesh's mind, and the other is the Spirit's mind], life and peace. Because the mind of the flesh is enmity toward God: for to the law of God it is not subject; for neither can it be; and they that in flesh are, God please can not [that is, cannot please God]. But ye are not in flesh, but in spirit, if indeed the Spirit of God dwells in you; but if any one the Spirit of Christ has not, he is not of him: but if Christ be in you, the body is dead, on account of sin, but the Spirit life [is] on account of righteousness.

"Our minds have consented to sin. We have felt the enticements of the flesh and our minds yielded, our minds consented and did the wills and the desires of the flesh, fulfilling the desires of the flesh and of the mind. The flesh leads and our minds have followed, and with the flesh the law of sin is served. When the mind can lead, the law of God is served. But as our minds have surrendered, yielded to sin, they have themselves become sinful and weak and are led away by the power of sin in the flesh.

"Now the flesh of Jesus Christ was our flesh and in it was all that is in our flesh—all the tendencies to sin that are in our flesh were in His flesh, drawing upon Him to get Him to consent to sin. Suppose He had consented to sin with His mind—what then? Then His mind would have been corrupted and then He would have become of like passions with us. But in that case He Himself would have been a sinner; He would have been entirely enslaved and we all would have been lost—everything would have perished.

"I will read now from the new Life of Christ, advance copy, upon this very point:

"It is true that Christ at one time said of himself, 'The prince of this world cometh, and hath nothing in me.' John 14:30. Satan finds in human hearts some point where he can gain a foothold; some sinful desire is cherished, by means of which his temptations assert their power.'

"Where does he start the temptation? In the flesh. Satan reaches the mind through the flesh; God reaches the flesh through the mind. Satan controls the mind through the flesh. Through this means—through the lusts of the flesh, the lusts of the eyes, the pride of life, and through ambition for the world and the honor and respect of men—through these things Satan draws upon us, upon our minds to get us to yield. Our minds respond and we cherish that thing. By this means his temptations assert their power. Then we have sinned. But until that drawing of our flesh is cherished, there is no sin. There is temptation, but not sin. Every man is tempted when he is drawn away thus and enticed, and when lust has conceived, when that desire is cherished, then it brings forth sin, and sin when it is finished bringeth forth death.

"Read farther now:

"'Some sinful desire [with us] is cherished, by means of which his temptations assert their power. But he could find nothing in the Son of God that would enable him to gain the victory. Jesus did not consent to sin. Not even by a thought could he be brought to yield to the power of temptation.'

"Thus you see that where the victory comes, where the battlefield is, is right upon the line between the flesh and the mind. The battle is fought in the realm of the thoughts. The battle against the flesh, I mean, is fought altogether and the victory won in the realm of the thoughts. Therefore, Jesus Christ came in just such flesh as ours but with a mind that held its integrity against every temptation, against every inducement to sin—a mind that never consented to sin—no, never in the least conceivable shadow of a thought.

"And by that means He has brought that divine mind to every man on earth. Therefore every man for the choosing and by choosing can have that divine mind that conquers sin in the flesh. Dr. Young's translation of 1 John 5:20 is: 'Ye know that the Son of God has come, and hath given us a mind.' The German says the same thing exactly and the Greek too—'has given us a mind.' To be sure he has. That is what He came for. We had the carnal mind, the mind that followed Satan and yielded to the flesh.

"What was it that enslaved Eve's mind? O, she saw that the tree was good for food. It was not good for any such thing. The appetite, the lusts of the flesh, the desires of the flesh, led her off. She took of the tree and did eat. The appetite led, and enslaved the mind—that is the mind of the flesh, and that is enmity against God; it comes from Satan. In Jesus Christ it is destroyed by the divine mind which He brought into the flesh. By this divine mind He put the enmity underfoot and kept it there. By this He condemned sin in the flesh. So there is our victory. In Him is our victory, and it is all in having that mind which was in Him.

"O, it is all told in the beginning. There came in this enmity, and Satan took man captive and enslaved the mind. God says, 'I will put enmity between thee and the woman and between thy seed and her seed.' Who was her seed? Christ. 'It [her seed] shall bruise thy head and thou shalt bruise his' head? No, sir. No, sir. 'Thou shalt bruise his heel.' All that Satan could do with Christ was to entice the flesh, to lay temptations before the flesh. He could not affect the mind of Christ. But Christ reaches the mind of Satan, where the enmity lies and where it exists and He destroys that wicked thing. It is all told there in the story in Genesis.

"The blessedness of it is, Satan can only deal with the flesh. He can stir up the desires of the flesh, but the mind of Christ stands there and says, No, no. The law of God is to be served and the body of flesh must come under.

"We shall have to follow this thought further. But even only so far there is blessing, there is joy, there is salvation in it for every soul. Therefore 'let this mind be in you, which was also in Christ Jesus.' That conquers sin in the sinful flesh. By his promise we are made partakers of the divine nature. Divinity and humanity are united once more when the divine mind of Jesus Christ by His divine faith abides in human flesh. **Let them be united in you and be glad and rejoice forevermore in it.**

"Thus you see the mind which we have is the flesh's mind. It is controlled by the flesh and it came to us from whom? Satan. Therefore it is enmity against God. And that mind of Satan is the mind of self, always self, in the place of God. Now Christ came to bring to us another mind than that. While we have Satan's mind, the flesh ruling, we serve the law of sin. God can reveal to us His law and we can consent that that is good and desire to fulfill it and make resolutions to do so and sign bargains and make contracts even, 'but I see another law in my members [in my flesh], warring against the law of my mind [against that desire, that wish of my mind, that delights in the law of God], and bringing me into captivity to the law of sin which is in my members. O wretched man that I am!' But Christ comes and brings another mind—the Spirit's mind—to us and gives us that. He gives us a mind and we have His mind by His Holy Spirit. Then and therefore with the mind—the Spirit's mind, the mind of Christ which He hath given us—the law of God is served. Thank the Lord.

"So see the difference. In the seventh of Romans there is described the man in whom the flesh rules and leads the mind astray, against the will of the man even. In the ninth chapter of 1 Corinthians, verses 26, 27, is described the man in whom the mind has control. This is the Christian. The mind has control of the body and the body is under, and he keeps it under. Therefore it is written in another place (Rom. 12:2):

"'Be not conformed to this world: but be ye transformed by the renewing of your mind.'

"And the Greek word is the same word exactly as that: 'If any man be in Christ, he is a new creation,' he is a new creature—not an old man changed over, but a new-made one. So this is not an old mind made over but a new-created mind. That is the mind of Christ wrought in us by the Spirit of God, giving us the mind of Christ and so making an entirely new mind in us and for us.

"This is shown in Romans, eighth chapter: 'They that are after the flesh do mind the things of the flesh,' because they do the works of the flesh, the mind follows sin that way. 'But they that after the Spirit [mind], the things of the Spirit.' And 'if any man have not the Spirit of Christ, he is none of his.' That which brings to us the mind of Jesus Christ is the Holy Ghost. Indeed, the Spirit of God brings Jesus Christ Himself to us. By the Holy Ghost the real presence of Christ is with us and dwells in us. Can He bring Christ to us without bringing the mind of Christ to us? Assuredly not. So then in the nature of things there is the mind of Christ which He came into the world to give us.

"Now see how this follows further and what it cost to do that and how it was done. This mind of the flesh is the minding of self. It is enmity against God and is controlled through the flesh. Jesus Christ came into this flesh Himself—the glorious One—He who made the worlds, the Word of God—was made flesh Himself and He was our flesh. And He, that divine One who was in heaven was in our sinful flesh. Yet that divine One, when in sinful flesh never manifested a particle of His divine self in resisting the temptations that were in that flesh but emptied Himself.

"We are here studying the same subject that we have been studying these three or four years, but God is leading us further along in the study of it, and I am glad. We have been studying for three or four years, 'Let this mind be in you which was also in Christ Jesus,' who emptied Himself. That mind must be in us in order for us to be emptied, for we cannot of ourselves empty ourselves. Nothing but divinity can do that. That is an infinite thing. Can the mind of Satan empty itself of self? No. Can the mind that is in us, that minding of self, empty itself of self? No. Self cannot do it. Jesus Christ, the divine One, the infinite One, came in His divine person in this same flesh of ours and never allowed His divine power, His personal self, to be manifested at all in resisting these temptations and enticements and drawings of the flesh.

"What was it, then, that conquered sin there and kept Him from sinning? It was the power of God the Father that kept Him. Now where does that touch us? Here. We cannot empty ourselves, but His divine mind comes into us and by that divine power we can empty ourselves of our wicked selves and then by that divine power the mind of Jesus Christ, of God the Father, comes to us and keeps us from the power of temptation. Thus Christ, emptying His divine self, His righteous self, brings to us the power by which we are emptied of our wicked selves. And this is how He abolished in His flesh the enmity and made it possible for the enmity to be destroyed in you and me.

"Do you see that? I know it takes close thinking, and I know too that when you have thought upon that and have got it clearly, then the mind cannot go any further. There we come face to face with the mystery of God itself, and human, finite intellect must stop and say, That is holy ground. That is beyond my measure. I can go no further. I surrender to God.

"[Question: Did not Christ depend on God to keep Him? Answer: Yes, that is what I am saying. That is the point.]

"Christ depended on the Father all the time. Christ Himself, who made the worlds, was all the time in that sinful flesh of mine and yours which He took. He who made the worlds was there in His divine presence all the time, but never did He allow Himself to appear at all or to do anything at all that was done. That was kept back, and when these temptations came upon Him, He could have annihilated them all with the assertion—in righteousness, of His divine self. But if He had done so, it would have ruined us. To have asserted Himself, to have allowed Himself to appear, even in righteousness, would have ruined us, because we who are only wicked never would have had anything before us then but the manifestation of self. Set before men who are only wicked, manifestation of self, even in divine righteousness, as an example to be followed and you simply make men that much more confirmed in selfishness and the wickedness of selfishness. Therefore, in order that we in our wicked selves might be delivered from our wicked selves, the divine One, the holy One, kept under, surrendered, emptied all the manifestation of His righteous self. And that does accomplish it. He accomplished it by keeping Himself back all the time and leaving everything entirely to the Father to hold Him against these temptations. He was Conqueror through the grace and power of the Father, which came to Him upon His trust and upon His emptying Himself of self.

"There is where you and I are now. There is where it comes to you and me. We are tempted, we are tried, and there is always room for us to assert ourselves and we undertake to make things move. There are suggestions which rise that such and such things are 'too much for even a Christian to bear,' and that 'Christian humility is not intended to go as far as that.' Some one strikes you on the cheek or breaks your wagon or tools or he may stone your tent or meetinghouse. Satan suggests, 'Now you send those fellows up. You take the law to them. Christians are not to bear such things as that in the world; that is not fair.' You answer Him: 'That is so. There is no use of that. We will teach those fellows a lesson.'

"Yes, and perhaps you do. But what is that? That is self-defense. That is self-replying. No. Keep back that wicked self. Let God attend to the matter. 'Vengeance is mine; I will repay, saith the Lord.' That is what Jesus Christ did. He was spat upon; he was taunted; he was struck upon the face; his hair was pulled; a crown of thorns was put upon his head and in mockery the knee was bowed, with 'Hail King of the Jews.' They blindfolded Him and then struck Him and cried: 'Prophesy, who is it that smote thee?' All that was put upon Him. And in His human nature He bore all that, because His divine self was kept back.

"Was there any suggestion to him, suppose you, to drive back that riotous crowd? to let loose one manifestation of His divinity and sweep away the whole wicked company? Satan was there to suggest it to Him, if nothing else. What did He do? He stood defenseless as the Lamb of God. There was no assertion of His divine self, no sign of it — only the man standing there, leaving all to God to do whatsoever He pleased. He said to Pilate: 'Thou couldst have no power at all against me, except it were given thee from above.' That is the faith of Jesus. And that is what the prophecy means when it says, 'Here are they that keep the commandments of God, and the faith of Jesus.' We are to have that divine faith of Jesus

Christ, which comes to us in the gift of the mind which He gives. That mind which He gives to me will exercise in me the same faith it exercised in Him. So we keep the faith of Jesus.

"So then there was He, by that self-surrender keeping back His righteous self and refusing ever to allow it to appear under the most grievous temptations—and the Spirit of Prophecy tells us that what was brought upon Him there in the night of His betrayal were the very things that were the hardest for human nature to submit to. But He, by the keeping back of His divine self, caused human nature to submit to it by the power of the Father, who kept Him from sinning. And by that means He brings us to that same divine mind, that same divine power, that when we shall be taunted, when we shall be stricken upon the face, when we shall be spat upon, when we shall be persecuted as He was—as shortly we shall be—that divine mind which was in Him being given to us will keep back our natural selves, our sinful selves and we will leave all to God. **Then the Father will keep us now in Him, as He kept us then in Him. That is our victory and there is how He destroyed the enmity for us. And in Him it is destroyed in us. Thank the Lord!**

"I will read a portion now from the Spirit of Prophecy that will help in the understanding of the subject.

"First from an article published in the Review and Herald of July 5, 1887. It is so good that I will read a few passages to go into the Bulletin with this lesson so that all can have it and so that all may know for certain that the steps we have taken in this study are exactly correct:

"'The apostle would call our attention from ourselves to the Author of our salvation. He presents before us His two natures, human and divine. Here is the description of the divine: 'Who, being in the form of God, thought it not robbery to be equal with God.' He was the 'brightness of his glory and the express image of his person.'

"Now of the human: He 'was made in the likeness of men: and being found in fashion as a man, he humbled himself, and became obedient unto death.' He voluntarily assumed human nature. It was his own act, and by his own consent. He clothed his divinity with humanity. He was all the while as God, but he did not appear as God. He veiled the demonstrations of Deity, which had commanded the homage and called forth the admiration of the universe of God. He was God while upon earth, but he divested himself of the form of God and in its stead took the form and fashion of man. He walked the earth as a man. For our sakes he became poor, that we through his poverty might become rich. He laid aside his glory and his majesty. He was God, but the glories of the form of God he for a while relinquished. Though he walked among men in poverty, scattering his blessings wherever he went, at his word legions of angels would surround their Redeemer and do him homage.

"When Peter, at the time of Christ's betrayal, resisted the officers and took the sword and raised it and cut off an ear of the servant of the high priest, Jesus said, Put up your sword. Don't you know that I could call twelve legions of angels?

"But he walked on the earth unrecognized, unconfessed with but few exceptions by his creatures. The atmosphere was polluted with sin and with curses instead of the anthems of praise. His lot was poverty and humiliation. As he passed to and fro on his mission of mercy to relieve the sick, to lift up the oppressed, scarce a solitary voice called him blessed, and the greatest of the nation passed him by with disdain.

"Contrast this with the riches of glory, the wealth of praise pouring forth from immortal tongues, the millions of rich voices in the universe of God in anthems of adoration. But he humbled himself, and took mortality upon him. As a member of the human family he was mortal, but as God he was the fountain of life to the world. He could, in his divine person, ever have withstood the advances of death and refused to come under its dominion, but he voluntarily laid down his life, that in doing so he might give life, and bring immortality to light. He bore the sins of the world and endured the penalty which rolled like a mountain upon his divine soul. He yielded up his life a sacrifice, that man might not eternally die. He died, not by being compelled to die, but by his own free will.'

"That is self-sacrifice; that is self-emptying.

"This was humility. The whole treasure of heaven was poured out in one gift to save fallen man. He brought into his human nature all the life-giving energies that human beings will need and must receive.

"And He brings it into my human nature yet, to your human nature, at our choice, by the Spirit of God bringing to us His divine presence and emptying us of ourselves and causing God to appear instead of self.

"Wondrous combination of man and God! He might have helped his human nature to stand the inroads of disease by pouring from his divine nature vitality and undecaying vigor to the human. But he humbled himself to man's nature. He did this that the Scripture might be fulfilled. And the plan was entered into by the Son of God, knowing all the steps in his humiliation that he must descend to make an expiation for the sins of a condemned, groaning world. What humility was this! It amazed angels. The tongue can never describe it; the imagination can never take it in.'

"But we can take in the blessed fact and enjoy the benefit of that to all eternity and God will give us eternity in which to take in the rest.

"The eternal Word consented to be made flesh. God became man.' He became man; what am I? A man. What are you? A man. He became ourselves and God with Him is God with us.

"'But He stepped still lower.' What, still lower than that yet? Yes, sir.

"'The man,' that is Christ, 'must humble himself as a man.' Because we need to humble ourselves, He not only humbled Himself as God, but when He became man, He humbled Himself as a man, so that we might humble ourselves to God. He emptied Himself as God and became man, and then as man He humbled Himself that we might humble ourselves. And all that we might be saved! In it is salvation. Shall we not take it and enjoy it day and night and be ever just as thankful as a Christian?

"But he stepped still lower. The man must humble himself as a man to bear insult, reproach, shameful accusations, and abuse. There seemed to be no safe place for him in his own territory. He had to flee from place to place for his life. He was betrayed by one of his disciples; he was denied by one of his most zealous followers. He was mocked; he was crowned with a crown of thorns. He was scourged. He was forced to bear the burden of the cross. He was not insensible to this contempt and ignominy. He submitted, but O, he felt the bitterness as no other being could feel it! He was pure, holy, and undefiled, yet arraigned as a criminal. The adorable Redeemer stepped down from the high exaltation. Step by step he humbled himself to die, but what a death! It was the most shameful, the most cruel—the death on the cross as a malefactor. He did not die as a hero in the eyes of the world, loaded with honors, as men die in battle. He died a condemned criminal, suspended between the heavens and the earth—died a lingering death of shame, exposed to the revilings and tauntings of a debased, crime-loaded, profligate multitude. 'All they that see me laugh me to scorn: they shoot out the lip, they shake the head.' Ps. 22:7. He was numbered with the transgressors and his kinsmen according to the flesh disowned him. His mother beheld his humiliation and he was forced to see the sword pierce her heart. He endured the cross, despised the shame. He made it of small account in consideration of the results he was working out in behalf of not only the inhabitants of this speck of a world, but the whole universe—every world which God had created.

"Christ was to die as man's substitute. Man was a criminal under sentence of death for transgression of the law of God as a traitor, a rebel; hence a substitute for man must die as a malefactor, because he stood in the place of the traitors, with all their treasured sins upon his divine soul. It was not enough that Jesus should die in order to meet the demands of the broken law; but he died a shameful death. The prophet gives to the world his words: 'I hid not my face from shame and spitting!'

"In consideration of this, can men have one particle of self-exaltation? As they trace down the life and humiliation and sufferings of Christ, can they lift their proud heads as though they were to bear no shame, no trials, no humiliation? **I say to the followers of Christ, Look to Calvary and blush for shame at your self-important ideas. All this humiliation of the Majesty of heaven was for guilty, condemned man. He went lower and lower in his humiliation, until there were no lower depths he could reach in order to lift up man from his moral defilement.**

"How low down were we then when, in order to lift us up from moral defilement He had to go step by step lower and lower until there were no lower depths He could reach? Think of it and see how low we were! All this was for you who are striving

for the supremacy, striving for human praise, for human exaltation — you who are afraid you will not receive all that praise, all that deference from human minds, that you think is your due! Is this Christ like?

"Let this mind be in you which was also in Christ Jesus. He died to make an atonement, and to be a pattern for every one who would be his disciple. Shall selfishness come into your hearts? and shall those who set not before them the pattern, Jesus, extol your merits? You have none, except as they come through Jesus Christ. Shall pride be harbored after you have seen Deity humbling himself, and then as man debasing himself, until as man there were no lower depths to which he could descend? Be astonished, O, ye heavens, and be amazed, O ye inhabitants of the earth, that such returns should be made to your Lord.

"What contempt, what wickedness, what formality, what pride, what efforts made to lift up man and glorify himself, when the Lord of glory humbled himself, agonized, and died the shameful death on the cross in our behalf.

"**Who is learning the meekness and lowliness of the pattern? Who is striving earnestly to master self? Who is lifting his cross and following Jesus? Who is wrestling against self-conceit? Who is setting himself in good earnest and with all his energies to overcome Satanic envyings, jealousies, evil-surmisings, and lasciviousness, cleansing the soul-temple from all defilements, and opening the door of the heart for Jesus to come in? Would that these words might have that impression on the mind that all who read them might cultivate the grace of humility, be self-denying, more disposed to esteem others better than themselves, having the mind and spirit of Christ to bear one another's burdens. O, that we might write deeply on our hearts, as we contemplate the great condescension and humiliation to which the Son of God descended, that we might be partakers of the divine nature.'**

"Now I read a few lines from the advance pages of the new Life of Christ.

"'In order to carry out the great work of redemption, the Redeemer must take the place of fallen man. Burdened with the sins of the world, he must go over the ground where Adam stumbled. He must take up the work just where Adam failed, and endure a test of the same character, but infinitely more severe than that which had vanquished him. It is impossible for man fully to comprehend Satan's temptations to our Saviour. Every enticement to evil which men find so difficult to resist, was brought to bear upon the Son of God in as much greater degree as his character was superior to that of fallen man.

"'When Adam was assailed by the tempter, he was without the taint of sin. He stood before God in the strength of perfect manhood, all the organs and faculties of his being fully developed and harmoniously balanced; and he was surrounded with things of beauty, and communed daily with the holy angels. What a contrast to this perfect being did the second Adam present, as he entered the desolate wilderness to cope with Satan. For four thousand years the race had been decreasing in size and physical strength, and deteriorating in moral worth; and in order to elevate fallen man, Christ must reach him where he stood. He assumed human nature, bearing the infirmities and degeneracy of the race. He humiliated himself to the lowest depths of human woe, that he might sympathize with man and rescue him from the degradation into which sin had plunged him.

"'For it became him for whom are all things, and by whom are all things, in bringing many sons unto glory, to make the Captain of their salvation perfect through sufferings.' Heb. 2:10. 'And being made perfect, he became the author of eternal salvation unto all them that obey him.' Heb. 5:9. 'Wherefore in all things it behooved him to be made like unto his brethren, that he might be a merciful and faithful high priest in things pertaining to God to make reconciliation for the sins of the people. For in that he himself hath suffered being tempted, he is able to succor them that are tempted.' Heb. 2:17, 18. 'We have not a high priest which cannot be touched with the feeling of our infirmities; but was in all points tempted like as we are, yet without sin.' Heb. 4:15.

"'It is true that Christ at one time said of himself, 'The prince of this world cometh, and hath nothing in me.' John 14:30. Satan finds in human hearts some point where he can gain a foothold; some sinful desire is cherished, by means of which his temptations assert their power. But he could find nothing in the Son of God that would enable him to gain the victory. Jesus did not consent to sin. Not even by a thought could He be brought to the power of Satan's temptations. Yet it is written of Christ that

He was tempted in all points like as we are. Many hold that from the nature of Christ is was impossible for Satan's temptations to weaken or overthrow him. Then Christ could not have been placed in Adam's position, to go over the ground where Adam stumbled and fell; he could not have gained the victory that Adam failed to gain. Unless he was placed in a position as trying as that in which Adam stood, he could not redeem Adam's failure. If man has in any sense a more trying conflict to endure than had Christ, then Christ is not able to succor him when tempted. Christ took humanity with all its liabilities. He took the nature of man with the possibility of yielding to temptation, and he relied upon divine power to keep him.

"'The union of the divine with the human is one of the most mysterious, as well as the most precious, truths of the plan of redemption. It is of this that Paul speaks when he says, 'Without controversy great is the mystery of godliness: God was manifest in the flesh.' 1 Tim. 3:16. While it is impossible for finite minds fully to grasp this great truth or fathom its significance, we may learn from it lessons of vital importance to us in our struggles against temptation. Christ came to the world to bring divine power to humanity, to make man a partaker of the divine nature.'

"You see, we are on firm ground all the way, so that when it is said that he took our flesh but still was not a partaker of our passions, it is all straight; it is all correct, because His divine mind never consented to sin. And that mind is brought to us by the Holy Spirit that is freely given unto us.

"'We know that the Son of God has come, and hath given us a mind' and 'we have the mind of Christ.' 'Let this mind be in you, which was also in Christ Jesus.'" 1895 GCB Sermon 17 A.T. Jones

12 Union With Christ in Death & Resurrection by A.T. Jones

"We will begin our study this evening with Rom. 7:25: 'With the mind I myself serve the law of God.' I repeat the expression that I made in the previous lesson—that it is in the realm of the thoughts where the law of God is served, where the contention against sin is carried on and the victory won.

"The lust of the flesh, the lust of the eye, and the pride of life—these tendencies to sin that are in the flesh, drawing upon us—in this is the temptation. But temptation is not sin. Not until the desire is cherished is there sin. But as soon as the desire is cherished, as soon as we consent to it and receive it into the mind and hold it there, then there is sin; and whether that desire is carried out in action or not, the sin is committed. In the mind, in fact, we have already enjoyed the desire. In consenting to it we have already done the thing so far as the mind itself goes. All that can come after that is simply the sensual part, the sense of enjoying the satisfaction of the flesh.

"This is shown in the Saviour's words in Matt. 5:27,28:

> *"'Ye have heard that it was said by them of old time, Thou shalt not commit adultery: but I say unto you that whosoever looketh on a woman to lust after her hath committed adultery with her already in his heart.'*

"Therefore the only place where the Lord could bring help and deliverance to us, is right in the place where the thoughts are, at the very root of the thing that is sin, the very point where the sin is conceived and where it begins. Consequently, when tempted and tried as He was—when He was spat upon, when they struck Him in the face and on the head in the trial in Jerusalem and in all His public ministry when the Pharisees, the Sadducees, the scribes, and the priests in their iniquity and hypocrisy, which He knew, were all doing everything they could to irritate Him and get Him stirred up—when He was constantly tried thus, His hand was never raised to return the blow. He never had to check any such motion, because not even the impulse to make any such motion was ever allowed. Yet He had our human nature in which such impulses are so natural. Why then did not these motions manifest themselves in our human nature in Him?

"For the reason that He was so surrendered to the will of the Father that the power of God through the Holy Spirit so worked against the flesh and fought the battle right in the field of the thoughts, never, in the subtlest form of the thought was there allowed any such thing to conceive. So that under all these insults and grievous trials He was just as calm, our human nature in Him was just as calm, as it was when the Holy Spirit in the form of a dove overshadowed Him on the banks of the Jordan.

"Now 'let this mind be in you.' It is not enough for a Christian to become all stirred up and say a few spiteful words or raise the hand in resentment and then say to Himself, 'O, I am a Christian; I must not say this or do that.' No. We are to be so submitted to the power of God and to the influence of the Spirit of God that our thoughts shall be so completely controlled that the victory shall be won already and not even the impulse be allowed. Then we shall be Christians everywhere and all the time under all circumstances and against all influences. But until we do reach that point, we are not sure that we shall show a Christian spirit under all circumstances and at all times and against all insults.

"As stated in the previous lesson, the things that were heaped upon Christ and which He bore were the very things that were the hardest for human nature to bear. And we, before we get through with the cause in which we are engaged are going to have to meet these very things that are hardest for human nature to bear, and unless we have the battle won already and are Christians indeed, we are not sure that we shall show the Christian spirit in these times when it is most needed. In fact, the time when the Christian spirit is most needed is all the time.

"Now in Jesus the Lord has brought to us just the power that will give us into the hand of God and cause us to be so submitted to Him that He shall so fully control every thought that we shall be Christians all the time and everywhere, 'bringing into captivity every thought to the obedience of Christ.'

"'The kingdom of God is within you.' Christ dwells within us and He is the King. The law of God is written upon the heart and that is the law of the kingdom. Where the King and the law of the kingdom are, there is the kingdom. In the inmost recesses, the secret chamber of the heart, at the very root, the fountain of the thought—there Christ sets up His throne; there the law of God is written by the Spirit; there the King asserts His authority and sets forth the principles of His government and allegiance to that [sic.] is Christianity. Thus at the very citadel of the soul, the very citadel of the thoughts, the very place, the only place, where sin can enter—there God sets up His throne; there He establishes His kingdom; there He puts His law, and the power to cause the authority of the law to be recognized and the principles of the law to be carried out in the life, and the result is peace only and all the time. That is the very thing that Christ hath brought to us, and which comes to us in the mind of Christ.

"Let us look at that a little further. When Christ had our human nature, He was there in His divine self but didn't manifest any of His divine self in that place. What did He do with His divine self in our flesh when He became ourselves? His divine self was always kept back—emptied—in order that our evil, satanic selves might be kept back—emptied. Now in the flesh He Himself did nothing. He says: 'Of mine own self I can do nothing.' He was there all the time. His own divine self, who made the heavens, was there all the time. But from beginning to end He Himself did nothing. Himself was kept back; He was emptied. Who, then did that which was done in Him? The Father that dwelleth in Me, 'He doeth the works,

He speaks the words'—Then who was it that opposed the power of temptation in Him in our flesh? The Father. It was the Father who kept Him from sinning. He was 'kept by the power of God' as we are to be 'kept by the power of God.' 1 Peter 1:5.

"He was our sinful selves in the flesh, and here were all these tendencies to sin being stirred up in His flesh to get Him to consent to sin. But He Himself did not keep Himself from sinning. To have done so would have been Himself manifesting Himself against the power of Satan, and this would have destroyed the plan of salvation, even though He had not sinned. And though at the cross the words were said in mockery, they were literally true: 'He saved others; Himself He cannot save.' Therefore He kept Himself entirely out. He emptied Himself, and by His keeping Himself back, that gave the Father an opportunity to come in and work against the sinful flesh and save Him and save us in Him.

"Sinners are separated from God, and God wants to come back to the very place from which sin has driven Him in human flesh. He could not come to us, in ourselves, for we could not bear His presence. Therefore Christ came in our flesh and the Father dwelt with Him. He could bear the presence of God in its fullness, and so God could dwell with Him in His fullness and this could bring the fullness of God to us in our flesh.

"Christ came in that sinful flesh but did not do anything of Himself against the temptation and the power of sin in the flesh. He emptied Himself and the Father worked in human flesh against the power of sin and kept Him from sinning.

"Now it is written of the Christian: 'Ye are kept by the power of God through faith.' That is done in Christ. We yield to Christ; Christ abides in us, giving us His mind. That mind of Christ enables our wicked self to be in the background. The mind of Christ—'let this mind be in you which was also in Christ Jesus'—puts our wicked selves beneath and keeps ourselves back and keeps us from asserting ourselves, for any manifestation of ourself is of itself sin. When the mind of Christ puts ourselves beneath, that gives the Father a chance to work with us and keep us from sinning. And thus God 'worketh in you, both to will and to do of his good pleasure.' Thus it is always the Father and Christ and ourselves. It is the

Father manifested in us through Christ, and in Christ. The mind of Christ empties us of our sinful selves and keeps us from asserting ourselves in order that God, the Father, may join Himself to us and work against the power of sin and keep us from sinning. Thus Christ 'is our peace, who hath made both [God and us] one, and hath broken down the middle wall of partition between us; having abolished in his flesh the enmity...for to make in himself of twain one new man, so making peace.' So it is always the Father and Christ and we; we, the sinners; God the sinless; Christ joining the sinless One to the sinful one and in Himself abolishing the enmity, emptying self in us, in order that God and we may be one, and thus make one new man, so making peace. And thus the peace of God which passeth all understanding shall keep your hearts and minds through, or in, Jesus Christ.

"Is it not a most blessed thing that the Lord Jesus has done that for us and so takes up His abode in us and so settles that question that there can be no more doubt that the Father will keep us from sinning than there is that He has kept Him from sinning already? No more doubt; because when Christ is there, He is there for the purpose of emptying self in us. And when ourselves are gone, will it be any very great difficulty for the Father to manifest Himself? When ourselves are kept from asserting ourselves there will be no difficulty for God to assert Himself in our flesh. That is the mystery of God: 'Christ in you, the hope of glory.' God manifest in the flesh. It is not simply Christ manifest in the flesh; it is God manifest in the flesh. For when Jesus came in the world Himself, it was not Christ manifest in the flesh; it was God manifest in the flesh, for 'he that hath seen me, hath seen the Father.'

"Christ emptied Himself in order that God might be manifest in the flesh, in sinful flesh, and when He comes to us and dwells in us, upon our choice, bringing to us that divine mind of His which is the mind that empties self wherever it goes, wherever it can find an entrance, wherever it can find any place to act, the mind of Christ is the emptying of self, is the abolishing of self, the destruction of self, the annihilation of self. Therefore, when by our choice that divine mind comes to us, the result is as certain that ourselves will be emptied as that the mind dwells in us. And as soon as that is done, God works fully and manifests Himself, in sinful flesh though it be. And that is victory. That is triumph.

"And thus with the mind we serve the law of God. The law is manifested, it is fulfilled, its principles shine in the life, because the life is the character of God manifest in human flesh, sinful flesh, through Jesus Christ. It seems to me that that thought ought to raise every one of us above all the power of Satan and of sin. It will do that as certainly as we surrender to that divine mind and let it abide in us as it abode in Him. It will do it.

"Indeed, the word to us all the time is, 'Arise, shine.' But we cannot raise ourselves; it is the truth and the power of God that is to raise us. But is not here the direct truth that will raise a man? Yes, sir; it will raise Him from the dead, as we shall find before we get done with this. But this thought was necessary to be followed through, that we may see how complete the victory is and how certain we are of it as surely as we surrender to Christ and accept that mind that was in Him. And thus always bear in mind that the battle is fought against sin in the realm of the thoughts and that the Victor, the Warrior, that has fought the battle there and won the victory there in every conceivable kind of contest—that same blessed One comes and sets up His throne at the citadel of the very imagination of the thought, the very root of the thought of the heart of the believing sinner. He sets up His throne there and plants the principles of His law there and reigns there. Thus it is that as sin hath reigned unto death, even so now in this way might grace reign. Did sin reign? Certainly. Did it reign with power? Assuredly. It reigned. It ruled. Well, as that has reigned, even so grace shall reign. Is grace, then, to reign as certainly, as powerfully in fact, as ever sin did? Much more, much more fully, much more abundantly, much more gloriously. Just as certainly as ever sin did reign in us, so certainly when we are in Jesus Christ the grace of God is to reign much more abundantly, 'That as sin hath reigned unto death, even so might grace reign through righteousness unto eternal life by Jesus Christ our Lord.' That being so, we can go on in victory unto perfection.

"From that height—for it is proper to call it a height—to which this truth raises us, we can go on enjoying, reading with gratitude, what we have in Him and receiving it in the fullness of the soul. But unless we have the Lord to take us to that height and seat us there and put us where He has possession of the citadel so that we are certain where He is and in that where we are, all these other things are vague, indefinite, and seem to be beyond us—sometimes almost within our reach and we long to get where we can really have hold on them and know the reality of them, but yet they are always just a little beyond our reach and we are unsatisfied. **But when we surrender fully, completely, absolutely, with no reservation, letting the whole world and all there is of it, go, then we receive that divine mind of His by the Spirit of God that gives to Him possession of that citadel, that lifts us to that height where all these other things are not simply within reach—O, no, they are in the heart and are a rejoicing in the life! We then in Him have them in possession and we know it and the joy of it is just what Peter said, 'unspeakable and full of glory.'**

"So then as the Lord has lifted us to this height and will hold us there, now let us go ahead and read and receive, as we read, what we have in Him. Begin with Romans 6:6. That is the scripture that comes most directly in connection with this particular thought that we have studied so far this evening. 'Knowing this.'—Knowing what? 'Knowing this, that our old man is crucified with him.' Good! In Jesus Christ, in His flesh, was not human nature, sinful flesh, crucified? Whose? Who was He? He was man; He was ourselves. Then whose sinful flesh, whose human nature, was crucified on the cross of Jesus Christ?—Mine. Therefore, as certainly as I have that blessed truth settled in my heart and mind, that Jesus Christ was man, human nature, sinful nature, and that He was myself in the flesh—as certainly as I have that, it follows just as certainly as that He was crucified on the cross, so was I. My human nature, myself there, was crucified there. Therefore I can say with absolute truth and the certainty and confidence of faith, 'I am crucified with Christ.' It is so.

"We hear people so many times say, 'I want self to be crucified.' Well, we turn and read the text to them, 'Knowing this, that our old man is crucified.' And they respond: 'Well, I wish it were so.' Turn to the next text and read, 'I am crucified with Christ.' It says I am. Who is? Are you? Still they answer, I don't see that I am. I wish it were so, but I cannot see how I am crucified and I cannot see how reading that there and saying that that is so will make it so.' But the word of God says so and it is so because it says so and it would be true and everlastingly effectual if that were all there is to it. But in this case it is so because it is so. God does not speak that word to make it so in us; He speaks that word because it is so in us, in Christ.

"In the first chapter of Hebrews you remember we had an illustration of this. God did not call Christ God to make Him God. No. He called Him God because He was God...He was God and when God called Him God, He did so because that is what He was. So in that double sense it is everlastingly so. It is so by 'two immutable things.'

"Now it is the same way here. Our old man is crucified, yet when God sets forth His word that it is so, we accepting that word and surrendering to it, it is so to each one who accepts it because the word has the divine power in it to cause it to be so. And by that means it would be everlastingly so, even if that were all there is to it. But that is not all there is to it, because in Jesus Christ human nature has been crucified on the cross, actually, literally, and that is my human nature, that is myself in Him that was crucified there. And therefore God sets down the record of everyone who is in Christ, 'He is crucified.' So that by the two immutable things, by the double fact, it is so. Therefore, we can say with perfect freedom, it is no boasting, it is not presumption in any sense; it is simply the confession of faith in Jesus Christ, 'I am crucified with Christ.' Is not He crucified? Then as certainly as I am with Him, am I not crucified with Him? The word of God says so. 'Our old man is crucified with Him?' Very good. Let us thank the Lord that that is so.

"What is the use, then, of our trying, longing, to get ourselves crucified, so that we can believe that we are accepted of God? Why, it is done, thank the Lord! In Him it is done. As certainly as the soul by faith sinks self in Jesus Christ and by that divine power which He has brought to us to do it, so certainly it is done as a divine fact. And it is only the genuine expression of faith to tell, to acknowledge, that divine fact that 'I am crucified with Christ.' Jesus sunk His divine self in our human nature and altogether was crucified. When we sink ourselves in Him, it is so still, because in Him only is it done. It is all in Him. We call attention to the thought we had in the lesson a few evenings ago, that it is not in Him in the sense of His being a receptacle to which we can go and take it out and apply it to ourselves. No. But it is in Him in the sense that it is all there and when we are in Him, when we go into the receptacle, when we sink into Him, we have it all in Him as we are in Him.

"Therefore, now let every soul of us say by the faith of Jesus Christ, 'Knowing this, that our old man is crucified with Him.' 'I am crucified with Christ: nevertheless I live, yet not I, but Christ liveth in me.' He is alive again. And because He lives, we live also. 'Nevertheless I live; yet not I, but Christ liveth in me: and the life which I now live in the flesh I live by the faith'—**in** the Son of God? 'the faith **of** the Son of God,'—that divine faith which He brought to human nature and which He gives to you and to me. We 'live by the faith of the Son of God who loved me, and gave himself for me.' Gal. 2:20. O, He loved Me! When He gave Himself in all His glory and all His wondrous worth for me, who was nothing, is it much that I should give myself to Him?

"But there is more of the verse. Rom. 6:6 still: 'Knowing this, that our old man is crucified with him, that the body of sin might be destroyed that henceforth we should not serve sin.' Good! In Him we have the victory, victory from the service of sin. There is victory over the service of sin, in this knowing that we are crucified with Him.

"Now I say that this blessed fact which we find in Him lifts us right to that place; yea, and the fact holds us in the place. That is so. There is a power in it. That is a fact. We will have occasion to see it more fully presently.

"When He was crucified, what followed? When He was nailed to the cross, what came next? He died. Now read in this same chapter, eighth verse: 'Now if we be dead with Christ'—well, what else can there be? As certainly as I am crucified with Him, I shall be dead with Him. Being crucified with Him, we shall be dead with Him.

"Dead with Him? Do we know that? Look back at the fourth verse. When He had been crucified and had died, what followed? He was buried—the burial of the dead. And what of us? Now, 'therefore, we are buried with him.' Buried with Him! Were we crucified with Him? Did we die with Him? Have the Father and Christ wrought out in human nature the death of sinful self? Yes. Whose? Mine.

"Then do you not see that all this is a gift of faith that is to be taken with everything else that God gives of faith? The death of the old man is in Christ, and in Him we have it and thank God for it. With Him the old man was crucified. With Him the old man died, and when He was buried, the old man was buried. My human, old, sinful self was crucified, died and was buried with Him. And with Him it is buried yet when I am in Him. Out of Him I have it not, of course. Every one that is outside of Him has none of this. In Him it is—in Him. And we receive it all by faith in Him.

"We are simply studying now the facts that we have in him, the facts which are given to us in Him and which are to be taken by faith. These are facts of faith.

"We thank the Lord that all this is literal fact—that our old man is crucified, dead, and buried with Him and that in Him we have that gift. In Him we have the gift and the fact of the death of the old man—the death of the human, sinful nature and the burial of it. And when that old thing is crucified and dead and buried, then the next verse—the seventh: 'He that is dead is freed from sin.'

"So then, knowing 'that our old man is crucified with him' that henceforth we should not serve sin, we are free from the service of sin. Brethren I am satisfied it is just as much our place day by day now to thank God for freedom from the service of sin as it is to breathe. I say it over. I say it is just as much our place, our privilege and our right to claim in Christ—in Him only and as we believe in Him—and to thank God for freedom from the service of sin as it is to breathe the breath that we breathe as we get up in the morning.

"How can I ever have the blessing and the benefit there is in that thing if I do not take the thing? If I am always hesitating and afraid that I am not free from the service of sin, how long will it take to get me free from the service of sin? That very hesitating, that very fear, is from doubt, is from unbelief, and is sin in itself. But in Him, when God has wrought out for us indeed freedom from the service of sin, we have the right to thank God for it and as certainly as we claim it and thank Him for it, we shall enjoy it. 'He that is dead is freed from sin' (margin, 'is justified from sin'). and it is in Him, and we have it as we are in Him by faith.

"Let us therefore read the first verse of the sixth of Romans:

"'What shall we say then? Shall we continue in sin that grace may abound? God forbid. How shall we that are dead to sin live any longer therein.'

"Can a man live on what he died of? No. Then when the man has died of sin, can he live in sin? can he live with sin? A man dies of delirium tremens or typhoid fever. Can he live on delirium tremens or typhoid fever, even if by a possibility he should be brought to live long enough to realize that he was there? The very thought of it would be death to him, because it killed him once. So it is with the man who dies of sin. The very appearance of it, the very bringing of it before him after that is death to him. If he has consciousness enough and life enough to realize that it is there, he will die of it again. He cannot live on what he died of.

"But the great trouble with many people is that they do not get sick enough of sin to die. That is the difficulty. They get sick perhaps of some particular sin and they want to stop that and 'want to die' to that and they think they have left that off. Then they get sick of some other particular sin that they think is not becoming to them—they cannot have the favor and the estimation of the people with that particular sin so manifest and they try to leave that off. But they do not get sick of sin—sin in itself, sin in the conception, sin in the abstract, whether it be in one particular way or another particular way. They do not get sick enough of sin itself to die to sin. When the man gets sick enough—not of sins but of sin, the very suggestion of sin, and the thought of sin—why you cannot get him to live in it any more. He cannot live in it; it killed him once. And he cannot live in what he died of.

"We have constantly the opportunity to sin. Opportunities to sin are ever presented to us. Opportunities to sin and to live in it are presented day by day. But it stands written: 'Always bearing about in the body the dying of the Lord Jesus.' 'I die daily.' As certainly as I have died to sin, the suggestion of sin is death to me. It is death to me in Him.

"Therefore, this is put in the form of a surprised, astonished question, 'How shall we, that are dead to sin, live any longer therein? Know ye not, that so many of us as were baptized into Jesus Christ were baptized into his death?' Baptism means baptism into His death.

"'Therefore we are buried with him by baptism into death; that like as Christ was raised up from the dead by the glory of the Father, even so we also should walk in newness of life.'

"Turn to Colossians. There was the word you remember that we had in Brother Durland's lesson one day. Col. 2:20:

"'Wherefore if ye be dead with Christ from the rudiments of the world [the elements of the world, worldliness, and this thing that leads to the world—the enmity], why, as though living in the world, are ye subject to the world?'

"That is simply speaking of our deliverance from the service of sin. It is simply saying, in other words, what is said in Rom. 6: 6, 'Our old man is crucified with him, that the body of sin might be destroyed, that henceforth we should not serve sin.' Why, as though living outside of Him are we still doing those same things? No, sir. Rom. 6:14, 'For sin shall not have dominion over you.' The man who is delivered from the domination of sin is delivered from the service of sin. In Jesus Christ it is a fact, too. So read on from Romans 6:6-14.

"'Knowing this, that our old man is crucified with him, that the body of sin might be destroyed, that henceforth we should not serve sin. For he that is dead is freed from sin. Now if we be dead with Christ, we believe that we shall also live with him.'

"Is He alive? Yes. Thank the Lord! Who died? Jesus died, and we are dead with Him. And He is alive, and we who believe in Him are alive with Him. That, however, will come more fully afterward.

"Knowing that Christ being raised from the dead, dieth no more; death hath no more dominion over him. For in that he died, he died unto sin once: but in that he liveth, he liveth unto God.

"Let us hold to this. Let us thank God this moment and henceforward, day by day, with every thought, 'I am crucified with Him.' As certainly as He is crucified, I am crucified; as certainly as He is dead, I am dead with Him; as certainly as He is buried, I was buried with Him; as certainly as He is risen, I am risen with Him, and henceforth I shall not serve sin. In Him we are free from the dominion of sin and from the service of sin. Thank the Lord for His unspeakable gift!'" 1895 GCB Lecture 18

13 The Necessity of Victory Over Defects of Character

The true gospel proclaims total deliverance from both the guilt and power of sin not merely as talk but as a victorious living experience in Christ. The translation-bound end-time living remnant-elect will have overcome every defect of character in the process of being sanctified unto perfection.

At initial conversion the kingdom of God sets up the divine government in the "spirit of the mind" with Christ as king. Thereafter, Christ must reign in the mind until **all** His enemies — all deep seated defects of character — have been put under His feet. When this work will have been completed there will be jubilee in the souls of every remnant believer and the remnant church.

Only when He "shall have put down all rule and authority" in the souls of His **remnant church** will Christ have the right to "put down all rule and authority" in the **world**!

> "Then cometh the end, when he shall have delivered up the kingdom to God, even the Father; when he shall have put down all rule and all authority and power. For he must reign, till he hath put all enemies under his feet. The last enemy that shall be destroyed is death. For he hath put all things under his feet. But when he saith all things are put under him, it is manifest that he is excepted, which did put

all things under him. And when all things shall be subdued unto him, then shall the Son also himself be subject unto him that put all things under him, that God may be all in all." 1 Cor 15:24-28

"That they all may be one; as thou, Father, art in me, and I in thee, that they also may be one in us: that the world may believe that thou hast sent me. And the glory which thou gavest me I have given them; that they may be one, even as we are one: I in them, and thou in me, that they may be made perfect in one; and that the world may know that thou hast sent me, and hast loved them, as thou hast loved me." John 17:21-23

"And the seventh angel sounded; and there were great voices in heaven, saying, The kingdoms of this world are become the kingdom of our Lord, and of his Christ; and he shall reign for ever and ever." Rev 11:15

Defects In The Character Must Be Overcome

"Nevertheless the foundation of God standeth sure, having this seal, The Lord knoweth them that are his. And, Let every one that nameth the name of Christ depart from iniquity. But in a great house there are not only vessels of gold and of silver, but also of wood and of earth; and some to honour, and some to dishonour. If a man therefore purge himself from these, he shall be a vessel unto honour, sanctified, and meet for the master's use, and prepared unto every good work." 2 Tim 2:19-21

"*"He that covereth his sins shall not prosper: but whoso confesseth and forsaketh them shall have mercy.'* Proverbs 28:13. If those who hide and excuse their faults could see how Satan exults over them, how he taunts Christ and holy angels with their course, they would make haste to confess their sins and to put them away. Through defects in the character, Satan works to gain control of the whole mind, and he knows that if these defects are cherished, he will succeed. Therefore he is constantly seeking to deceive the followers of Christ with his fatal sophistry that it is impossible for them to overcome. But Jesus pleads in their behalf His wounded hands, His bruised body; and He declares to all who would follow Him: *'My grace is sufficient for thee.'* 2 Corinthians 12:9. *'Take My yoke upon you, and learn of Me; for I am meek and lowly in heart: and ye shall find rest unto your souls. For My yoke is easy, and My burden is light.'* Matthew 11:29, 30. Let none, then, regard their defects as incurable. God will give faith and grace to overcome them." GC 489

"Let church-members bear in mind that the fact that their names are registered on the church books will not save them. They must show themselves approved of God, workmen that need not to be ashamed. Day by day they are to build their characters in accordance with Christ's directions. They are to abide in him, constantly exercising faith in him. Thus they will grow up to the full stature of men and women in Christ,—wholesome, cheerful, grateful Christians, led by God, step by step, into clearer and still clearer light.

"Those who do not gain this experience will be among the ones whose voices will one day be raised in the bitter lamentation, 'The harvest is past, the summer is ended, and my soul is not saved. Why did I not flee to the stronghold for refuge? Why have I trifled with my soul's salvation, and done despite to the Spirit of grace?'

"Among those to whom fearful disappointment will come at the day of final reckoning will be those who have been outwardly religious, who have apparently lived Christian lives, but who have woven self into all that they do. They have prided themselves on their morality, their influence, their ability to stand in a higher position than others, their knowledge of the truth. They think that these will win for them the commendation of Christ. 'Lord,' they say, 'we have eaten and drunk in thy presence, and thou hast taught in our streets.' 'Have we not prophesied in thy name? and in thy name have cast out devils? and in thy name done many wonderful works?'

"But the Saviour says, *'I never knew you: depart from me.'* *'Not every one that saith unto me, Lord, Lord, shall enter into the kingdom of heaven; but he that doeth the will of my Father which is in heaven.'*

"There is no discussion; the time for that is past. The irrevocable sentence has been pronounced. They are shut out from heaven by their own unfitness for its companionship.

"Those who have bowed to the idols of the world will gain no comfort from them in that great day when every one will be rewarded or punished according to his works. But Omnipotence will deal justly. Those who have made Christ their refuge will find that he lives, and that he is conqueror. He will be their defense." R&H Nov 24, 1904

"Sin is a hateful thing. It marred the moral beauty of a large number of the angels. It entered our world, and well-nigh obliterated the moral image of God in man. But in his great love God provided a way whereby man might regain the position from which he fell in yielding to the tempter. Christ came to stand at the head of humanity, to work out in our behalf a perfect character. Those who receive him are born again. *'As many as received him, to them gave he power to become the sons of God.'*

"Christ saw humanity, through the working of the mighty growth of sin, demoniacally possessed by the prince of the power of the air, and putting forth gigantic strength in exploits of evil. But He saw also that a mightier power was to meet and conquer Satan. *'Now is the judgment of this world,'* He said; *'Now shall the prince of this world be cast out.'* He saw that if human beings believed in Him, they would be given power against the host of fallen angels, whose name is legion. Christ strengthened His own soul by the thought that by the wonderful sacrifice which He was about to make, the prince of this world was to be cast out, and men and women placed where, through the grace of God, they would regain what they had lost.

"What does the Lord require of his blood-bought heritage?— The sanctification of the whole being, — purity like the purity of Christ, perfect conformity to the will of God. My brethren and sisters, God requires this of us. Into the holy city there can enter nothing that defileth, or maketh a lie. God's word to us is, *'I am the Almighty God; walk before me, and be thou perfect.' 'Ye shall be holy unto me: for I the Lord am holy, and have severed you from other people, that ye should be mine.' 'Ye are bought with a price: therefore glorify God in your body, and in your spirit, which are God's.' 'In him dwelleth all the fulness of the Godhead bodily. And ye are complete in him, which is the head of all principality and power.'* He *'gave himself for us, that he might redeem us from all iniquity, and purify unto himself a peculiar people, zealous of good works.'*

"We can, we can, reveal the likeness of our divine Lord. We can know the science of spiritual life. We can honor our Maker. But do we do it? O, what an illustrious example we have in the life that Christ lived on this earth! He has shown us what we can accomplish through co-operation with divinity. We are to seek for the union of which he speaks when he says, *'Abide in me, and I in you.'* This union is deeper, stronger, truer, than any other union, and is productive of all good. Those who are thus united to the Saviour are controlled by his will, and are moved by his love to suffer with those who suffer, to rejoice with those who rejoice, to feel a deep sympathy for every one in weakness, sorrow, or distress.

"Higher than the highest human thought can reach is God's ideal for his children. He wants our minds to be clear, our tempers sweet, our love abounding. Then the peace that passeth knowledge will flow from us to bless all with whom we come in contact. The atmosphere surrounding our souls will be refreshing.

"But how few there are who are making determined efforts to reach this ideal. Satan is trying to keep the people of God dwarfed, feeble, un-Christlike. And too often he is successful.

In our churches there are many who have not the spirit of the Master, many who act as if they were in the world merely to please themselves. They forget that the enemy is assailing all who profess to be children of God, trying to overcome them, so that they will disappoint and dishonor the Saviour. They forget that the purity and unselfishness that characterized the life of Christ must characterize their lives, else in the day of God they will be found wanting, and will hear from his lips the irrevocable sentence, *'Cast ye the unprofitable servant into outer darkness; there shall be weeping and gnashing of teeth.'* R&H Nov 24, 1904

Sanctified By The Truth In Daily Conversion Through Abiding In Christ

"I am the true vine, and my Father is the husbandman. Every branch in me that beareth not fruit he taketh away: and every branch that beareth fruit, he purgeth it, that it may bring forth more fruit. Now ye are clean through the word which I have spoken unto you. Abide in me, and I in you. As the branch cannot bear fruit of itself, except it abide in the vine; no more can ye, except ye abide in me." John 15:1-4

Sanctification Through the Truth

"It is through the truth, by the power of the Holy Spirit, that we are to be sanctified,–transformed into the likeness of Christ. And in order for this change to be wrought in us, there must be an unconditional, whole-hearted acceptance of the truth, an unreserved surrender of the soul to its transforming power.

"Our characters are by nature warped and perverted. Through the lack of proper development they are wanting in symmetry. With some excellent qualities are united objectionable traits, and through long indulgence wrong tendencies become second nature, and many persons cling tenaciously to their peculiarities. Even after they profess to accept the truth, to yield themselves to Christ, the same old habits are indulged, the same self-esteem is manifested, the same false notions entertained. Although such ones claim to be converted, it is evident that they have not yielded themselves to the transforming power of the truth.

"These things are not only harming their own souls, but are misleading others, who look to them as representatives of the truths which they profess to believe. Here we may see why some of our ministers as well as laymen have not greater power. They have not made an entire surrender to God. They do not realize the sinfulness of clinging to their own ways, following their own ideas, which are crude and narrow, and without symmetry. They hold tenaciously to the theory of the truth, and try to present it to others, but it is so beclouded by their own peculiarities that its brightness is obscured; it appears unattractive, and too often is refused.

"Those who accept unpopular truth must receive it in the face of many opposing influences. Tradition, custom, and prejudice barricade their souls against the light. The advocates of truth must give evidence in their own character of its reforming, transforming power, or their labors will have little effect.

"Again: those who do accept the truth naturally expect that the one who presents it to them is right in his ideas of general principles and of what constitutes Christian character. When associated with him, they incline to do as he does. If his practices are wrong, they almost imperceptibly become partakers of the evil. His defects are reproduced in their religious experience. Often, through their love and reverence for him, some objectionable feature of his character is even copied by them as a virtue. If the one who is thus misrepresenting Christ could know what harm has been wrought by the faults of character which he has excused and cherished, he would be filled with horror.

"All who receive the truth are to stand as its representatives and advocates; the same responsibility rests in a degree upon all members of the church, whether ministers or laymen. Every soul who receives the truth should make the fullest possible surrender of himself to God,–a surrender represented as falling upon the Rock and being broken. Our old habits, our hereditary and cultivated traits of character, must all be yielded to the transforming power of Christ if we would become vessels unto honor, meet for the Master's use, prepared unto every good work.

"As the Comforter shall come, and reprove you of sin, of righteousness, and of judgment, be careful lest you resist the Spirit of God, and thus be left in darkness, not knowing at what you stumble. Be willing to discern what it shall reveal to you. Yield up your self-will, the long idolized habits peculiar to yourself, that you may receive the principles of truth. Thus you become a branch of the True Vine, and you will not bear wild grapes or thorn-berries, but rich clusters of precious fruit, just like that which grows upon the parent stock.

"Said Christ, "Every branch in me that beareth not fruit he taketh away: and every branch that beareth fruit, he purgeth it, that it may bring forth more fruit." Why prune the branch that is already bearing fruit? Because its tendrils are fastening upon earthly rubbish, too much of its strength has gone to the growth of the stem and leaves, and too little to the production of fruit. The vine must be cut away, the tendrils that bind it earthward must be severed. It must be rightly directed. Then it will produce more fruit, and of more precious quality.

"John says, *'The light'*—Christ—*'shineth in darkness,'* that is, in the world, *'and the darkness comprehended it not...But as many as received him, to them gave he power to become the sons of God, even to them that believe on his name: which were born, not of blood, nor of the will of the flesh, nor of the will of man, but of God.'* The reason why the unbelieving world are not saved is that they do not choose to be enlightened. The old nature, born of blood and the will of the flesh, cannot inherit the kingdom of

God. The old ways, the hereditary tendencies, the former habits, must be given up; for grace is not inherited. The new birth consists in having new motives, new tastes, new tendencies. Those who are begotten unto a new life by the Holy Spirit, have become partakers of the divine nature, and in all their habits and practices, they will give evidence of their relationship to Christ. When men who claim to be Christians retain all their natural defects of character and disposition, in what does their position differ from that of the worldling? They do not appreciate the truth as a sanctifier, a refiner. They have not been born again.

"The command, *'Be ye therefore perfect, even as your Father which is in heaven is perfect,'* would never have been given, if every provision had not been made whereby we may become as perfect in our sphere as God is in his. We are to be ever advancing from light to a greater light, holding fast what we have already received, and praying for more. Thus we shall never be left in darkness.

"Let none feel that their way needs no changing. Those who decide thus are not fitted to engage in the work of God, for they will not feel the necessity of pressing constantly toward a higher standard, making continual improvement. None can walk safely unless they are distrustful of self, and are constantly looking to the word of God, studying it with willing heart to see their own errors, and to learn the will of Christ, and praying that it may be done in and by and through them. They show that their confidence is not in themselves, but in Christ. They hold the truth as a sacred treasure, able to sanctify and refine, and they are constantly seeking to bring their words and ways into harmony with its principles. They fear and tremble lest something savoring of self shall be idolized, and thus their defects be reproduced in others who confide in them. They are always seeking to subdue self, to put away everything that savors of it, and to supply the place with the meekness and lowliness of Christ. They are looking unto Jesus, growing up into him, gathering from him light and grace, that they may diffuse the same to others.

"The truth, the grace of Christ, received into the soul never rests content with its own existence. It is always gathering, diffusing, and increasing by diffusing. It is an active, working principle. As long as there are sinners to be saved, grace and love and truth are seeking for them. Jesus said: *'I, if I be lifted up from the earth, will draw all men unto me.'* We are to be laborers together with him; but our work is to lift up Christ. He alone can draw men unto him.

"Never think that even when you do your best, you are, of yourself, capable of winning souls to Christ. You must cultivate the habit of discerning a power beyond that which can be seen with human vision—a power that is constantly at work upon the hearts of men. When you approach the stranger, when you stand face to face with the impenitent, the afflicted, the soul-needy, the Lord is by your side if you have indeed given yourself to him. He makes the impression on the heart. But you may be the instrument for his gracious work. You cannot reach hearts with a mere form of words, a parrot-like repetition of set phrases. What you say must be the expression of a personal experience: If you cheer hearts with words of courage and hope, it will be because the grace and love of God are to you a living reality. It is God's impress that these souls are to receive, not your own. But if the worker has not himself been refined, transformed, he cannot present the truth with a freshness, a force, a power, that awakens responsive feelings in those who hear the word of life.

"It is true that some will be found who will accept the truth on its own merits, notwithstanding the defects of the one who presents it to them. Though himself unsanctified in heart, he may bring forward conclusive evidence in favor of the truth; and those upon whose hearts the Spirit of God has been moving, leading them to hunger and thirst for truth, will by the same Spirit be led to accept the truth when it is presented. It was not the man who made the impression, but the Comforter, the Spirit of truth, that Christ promised to send, to lead his disciples into all truth.

But how much more might be accomplished in winning souls, if all who present the truth were instruments for the working of the Spirit of God.

"Those to whom the message of truth is spoken, seldom ask, "Is it true?" But, "Who are the men that present these doctrines?" They judge of the truth by the character of its advocates. Multitudes estimate it by the numbers who accept it; and the question is often asked, as of old, "Have any of the rulers or the Pharisees believed?" We cannot boast of large numbers, or of the patronage of the wealthy, or the great in the world's estimation. Here is not the source of our strength. God declared to Israel, through Moses, "The Lord did not set his love upon you, nor choose you, because ye were more in number than any people; for ye were the fewest of all people." The advocates of truth must hide in Jesus; He is their greatness, their power and efficiency. They must love souls as he loved them, be obedient as he was, be courteous, full of sympathy. **They should war with all their power against the least defect of character in themselves. They must represent Jesus. In every act let him appear.** R&H April 12, 1892.

Appeal

"How is it with those who are here to-day? Are there not some who believe not, who have no real foundation for their faith? Are there not some who would find in the hour of temptation that their hope was but sliding sand? We should seek to know the character of our title to the heavenly treasure. God knows who among us will turn aside and give heed to seducing spirits. He knows those who are cherishing defects of character, and permitting these defects to have an overcoming power upon them, until they shall be led, as was Judas, to betray their Lord.

"The words that Jesus uttered proved the hearts of many who professed to be his followers, and *'from that time many of his disciples went back, and walked no more with him. Then said Jesus unto the twelve, Will ye also go away? Then*

Simon Peter answered him, Lord, to whom shall we go? thou hast the words of eternal life. And we believe and are sure that thou art that Christ, the Son of the living God.'

"Christ brought a testing truth to bear upon his disciples at that time, and had they borne the test, they would have manifested the faith that makes the soul a partaker of the divine nature; but the test found their faith an empty profession, and at the suggestion of the enemy they were turned against their Lord. The difficulties, the self-denials, seemed more than they could surmount, and they walked no more with him.

"We shall all be tested by trial and temptation, and we shall be able to endure only by having genuine faith, by having root in ourselves. It will not do for us to depend upon others. We must know that we have a hold from above. May God help us to realize the importance of examining our hearts to see whether or not we are in the faith. There are many who will fail because they do not gather every ray of light emanating from the word of life; they do not cherish the divine precepts, and dwell upon the precious promises of God. If they did this, fruits of righteousness would appear in their life, and every day they would be growing stronger and stronger, and more and more like Christ.

"Our bodies are composed of what we eat; and by partaking of nourishing food, we have good blood, firm muscles, and vigorous health. So in our spiritual nature, we are composed of what we dwell upon. If we take the lessons which Christ has given us, and make them practical, living out his instructions, we are then eating the flesh and drinking the blood of our Saviour, and becoming more and more like him in life and character. In this way we come to know that his going forth is prepared as the morning. How is that? When the day dawns, the light is faint and subdued; but as the sun rises, its light increases and strengthens, until its rays reach the perfect day. This is the way in which the Christian's light is to increase. We are to know more of Christ to-day than we knew yesterday;

we are to grow in grace and in the knowledge of our Lord and Saviour; we are to trust him more in trial and difficulty, looking to him as the author and finisher of our faith. In sorrow and temptation we are to realize that he is touched with the feeling of our infirmities; that he was a man of sorrows and acquainted with grief; that he was wounded for our transgressions, and by his stripes we are healed.

"Christ has promised, *'Him that cometh to me I will in no wise cast out.'* He will hear and answer our prayers, and faith appropriates the rich promises of God, believing they are for us. As we accept the promises of God, we grow stronger in faith, and find the word of the Lord fulfilled as he has spoken it. We may feel our weakness and unworthiness, and because of this, realize our dependence upon God. Every one of us can have a rich experience in the things of God if we will utterly forsake our sin and submit ourselves to God. O, how can we cherish impurity in the soul when Christ has died for us, that we may become partakers of the divine nature, and escape the corruption that is in the world through lust? We are to be sanctified through the truth, and this sanctification is not the work of a moment, but of a life-time. We must all learn to lean upon Jesus; for the time will come when we shall be scattered, and we cannot lean upon one another. Christ is ready to give us the help we need. The Bible is full of precious treasure, but we must dig for it as did the man who purchased the field of treasure. In this way we shall learn what it is to have living faith. Many are enfeebling the mind by the reading of stories and novels, and are losing their relish for the word of God. They are becoming mental inebriates, and will be unable to look at the solemn questions of life and destiny in the right light, unless they put away this practice. Search the Scriptures, and know what is truth. Lean upon God, and know what is living faith, and live by every word that proceedeth out of the mouth of God. RH April 14, 1891

14 The Functional Anatomy of Deep-Seated Defects

Ignorance of Satan's devices gives him an advantage, but when we know his devices and submit to God, Satan cannot get any advantage over us.

> *"Submit yourselves therefore to God. Resist the devil, and he will flee from you. Draw nigh to God, and he will draw nigh to you. Cleanse your hands, ye sinners; and purify your hearts, ye double minded." James 4:7,8*

> *"Lest Satan should get an advantage of us: for we are not ignorant of his devices." 2 Cor 2:11*

> *"Be sober, be vigilant; because your adversary the devil, as a roaring lion, walketh about, seeking whom he may devour: Whom resist stedfast in the faith, knowing that the same afflictions are accomplished in your brethren that are in the world. But the God of all grace, who hath called us unto his eternal glory by Christ Jesus, after that ye have suffered a while, make you perfect, stablish, strengthen, settle you." 1 Peter 5:8-10*

> *"There hath no temptation taken you but such as is common to man: but God is faithful, who will not suffer you to be*

tempted above that ye are able; but will with the temptation also make a way to escape, that ye may be able to bear it."
1 Cor 10:13

"There is earnest warfare before all who would subdue the evil tendencies that strive for the mastery" GC 490

"Through defects in the character, Satan works to gain control of the whole mind and he knows that if these defects are cherished, he will succeed." GC 489

But God has given us, in Christ, the weapons for successful warfare.

"Then he answered and spake unto me, saying, This is the word of the LORD unto Zerubbabel, saying, Not by might, nor by power, but by my spirit, saith the LORD of hosts."
Zech 4:6

"For though we walk in the flesh, we do not war after the flesh: (For the weapons of our warfare are not carnal, but mighty through God to the pulling down of strong holds;) Casting down imaginations, and every high thing that exalteth itself against the knowledge of God, and bringing into captivity every thought to the obedience of Christ;"
2 Cor 10:3-5 KJV

Let us read these verses as rendered in the JB Phillips Translation of the New Testament:

"The truth is that, although of course we lead normal human lives, the battle we are fighting is on the spiritual level. The very weapons we use are not those of human warfare but powerful in God's warfare for the destruction of the enemy's strongholds. Our battle is to bring down every deceptive fantasy and every imposing defence that men erect against the true knowledge of God. We even fight to capture every thought until it acknowledges the authority of Christ."
2 Cor 10:3-5 JB Phillips

Definition Of A Satanic Stronghold

What is a satanic stronghold?

A satanic stronghold is a particular **way of thinking** which holds us in **bondage**. We can go a little further and say that a satanic stronghold is a **defect of character** which is **deep-seated** and which **produces** negative or **unChristlike** behaviour under **provocation** i.e. under temptation; trial or adversity.

We have learnt already that Satan works through such defects, such strongholds, to gain control of the whole mind. It is, therefore, of the utmost importance for us to understand how these defects or strongholds are built and how Satan works through them. In other words we must understand the structure (anatomy) and function of the satanic strongholds or defects of character.

Structure Of Satanic Strongholds In The Mind

Satanic strongholds or defects of character are **wrong ways of thinking, systems of thought, thought patterns, thought circuits** which have been built-in deep-down in the mind. There are some things we must know about them.

1. The **first** fact to grasp about any defect of character is that it is **SELF-CENTRED, not** Christ centred.

2. The **second** fact to know is that a defect of character, a satanic stronghold in the mind, is made up of **error.** There are two distinct **types** of error, one type is **doctrinal** error, the other type is **behavioural** or character error. By **doctrinal error** we mean that the person **believes** a **false** doctrine. By **behavioural error** we mean that the person has a **wrong way** of behaving built into the mind, into the thinking mechanism. As we shall discover, later on, these two types of error, though interrelated, involve different areas of the brain.

3. The **third** fact to understand is that a defect of character, a satanic stronghold in the mind, is a way of thinking which is **negative**. By **negative** we mean that it is **not** in harmony with the principles of Agape love as enunciated by Paul in 1 Corinthians 13 and by Jesus in the sermon on the mount in Matthew 5 through 7. Or to put it simply, a satanic

stronghold, a character defect, is a way of thinking which **opposes** the word of God and the love of God.

4. The fourth fact to know is that defects of character are **motivated** by **fear.**

5. The **fifth** fact to understand is that such defects are usually hidden deep down in the mind. They are not usually observed when things are going smoothly or to the person's liking.

6. The **sixth** and last fact to discern is that sooner or later such defects are **exposed** when they **trigger** sinful, **unChristlike** behaviour under some provocation which may be real or imagined!

Let us summarize the aforementioned 6 facts by drawing a circuit diagram of a satanic stronghold in the mind, a character defect:

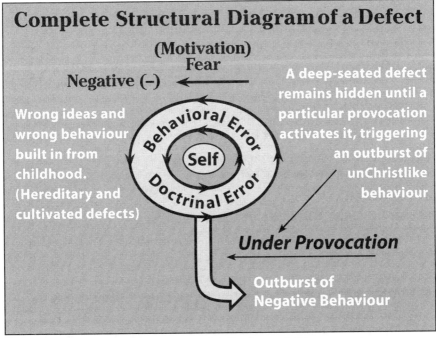

Circuit Diagram of a Defect of Character

Having examined the structure of a defect, a satanic stronghold, let us look now at the weapons of our warfare.

The Weapons of Our Spiritual Warfare

"And he said to them all, If any man will come after me, let him deny himself, and take up his cross daily, and follow me. For whosoever will save his life shall lose it: but whosoever will lose his life for my sake, the same shall save it." Luke 9:23,24

"For even Christ pleased not himself;" Romans 15:3

---

1 **The Principle of the Cross is the Weapon against Self-Centeredness, the spiritual weapon of self-denial.**

The principle of self-sacrificing love is the foundation principle of God's government. It is in fact the **law of life** for the universe and it was fully revealed at the cross.

"Both the redeemed and the unfallen beings will find in the cross of Christ their science and their song. It will be seen that the glory shining in the face of Jesus is the glory of self-sacrificing love. In the light from Calvary it will be seen that the law of self-renouncing love is the law of life for earth and heaven; that the love which "seeketh not her own" has its source in the heart of God; and that in the meek and lowly One is manifested the character of Him who dwelleth in the light which no man can approach unto." DA 19, 20

"At the birth of Jesus, Satan knew that One had come with a divine commission to dispute his dominion. He trembled at the angel's message attesting the authority of the newborn King. Satan well knew the position that Christ had held in heaven as the Beloved of the Father. That the Son of God should come to this earth as a man filled him with amazement and with apprehension. He could not fathom the mystery of this great sacrifice. His selfish soul could not understand such love for the deceived race." DA 115

"To many minds a deep mystery surrounds the fate of John the Baptist. They question why he should have been left to languish and die in prison. The mystery of this dark providence our human vision cannot penetrate; but it can never shake our confidence in God when we remember that John was but a sharer in the sufferings of Christ. All who follow Christ will wear the crown of sacrifice. They will surely be misunderstood by selfish men, and will be made a mark for the fierce assaults of Satan. **It is this principle of self-sacrifice that his kingdom is established to destroy, and he will war against it wherever manifested."** DA 223

---

2 The Truth is the Weapon Against Error

Doctrinal truth is received by studying Bible truth, allowing scripture to interpret scripture.

"Sanctify them through thy truth: thy word is truth."
John 17:17

"And ye shall know the truth, and the truth shall make you free." John 8:32

"But if we walk in the light, as he is in the light, we have fellowship one with another, and the blood of Jesus Christ his Son cleanseth us from all sin." 1 John 1:7

"But God hath revealed them unto us by his Spirit: for the Spirit searcheth all things, yea, the deep things of God. For what man knoweth the things of a man, save the spirit of man which is in him? even so the things of God knoweth no man, but the Spirit of God. Now we have received, not the spirit of the world, but the spirit which is of God; that we might know the things that are freely given to us of God." 1 Cor 2:10-12

Behavioural truth is learnt by studying the life, the character, of Christ and therefore of God.

"Take my yoke upon you, and learn of me; for I am meek and lowly in heart: and ye shall find rest unto your souls."
Matt 11:29

"But we all, with open face beholding as in a glass the glory of the Lord, are changed into the same image from glory to glory, even as by the Spirit of the Lord." 2 Cor 3:18

Behavioural errors, wrong ways of behaving or reacting under provocation, are learnt from early childhood and are the most deeply embedded of all character defects. They include some of the most difficult to overcome. Here are some examples: **anger; impatience; retaliation; an unforgiving spirit; envy; jealously; being unduly sensitive; pride; misery; fretfulness; discontent; inability to express love; inability to admit wrong; strife for the supremacy; lust; covetousness.** These defects usually require the application of **all** the weapons of our warfare in order to conquer them. But especially do they require the deeper death to self by the deeper, daily experience of the principle of the cross and diligently studying the **true** message of God's character.

---

3 Thinking Positively is the Weapon Against Negative Direction of Thoughts.

It was Solomon who said that as a man thinks in his heart so is he (Proverbs 23:7). Let us not dwell on the negative. God wants us to be positive, happy, overcoming people.

"And let us not be weary in well doing: for in due season we shall reap, if we faint not." Gal 6:9

"Why art thou cast down, O my soul? and why art thou disquieted in me? hope thou in God: for I shall yet praise him for the help of his countenance." Psalm 42:5

"When thou passest through the waters, I will be with thee; and through the rivers, they shall not overflow thee: when thou walkest through the fire, thou shalt not be burned; neither shall the flame kindle upon thee." Isa 43:2

"There is therefore now no condemnation to them which are in Christ Jesus, who walk not after the flesh, but after the Spirit."
Romans 8:1

"Be careful for nothing; but in every thing by prayer and supplication with thanksgiving let your requests be made known unto God. And the peace of God, which passeth all understanding, shall keep your hearts and minds through Christ Jesus. Finally, brethren, whatsoever things are true, whatsoever things are honest, whatsoever things are just, whatsoever things are pure, whatsoever things are lovely, whatsoever things are of good report; if there be any virtue, and if there be any praise, think on these things." Phil 4:6-8

This is how it reads in the JB Phillips translation:

"Delight yourselves in God, yes, find your joy in Him at all times. Have a reputation for gentleness, and never forget the nearness of your Lord. Don't worry over anything whatever; tell God every detail of your needs in earnest and thankful prayer, and the peace of God, which transcends human understanding, will keep constant guard over your hearts and minds as they rest in Christ Jesus. Here is a last piece of advice. If you believe in goodness and if you value the approval of God, fix your minds on the things which are holy and right and pure and beautiful and good." Phil 4:6-8

Always remember these three principles:

i) Our sufficiency is of God not self.

"Not that we are sufficient of ourselves to think any thing as of ourselves; but our sufficiency is of God;" 2 Cor 3:5

ii) Do not lose heart, do not give up, exercise faith through prayer!

"For which cause we faint not; but though our outward man perish, yet the inward man is renewed day by day." 2 Cor 4:16

"And he spake a parable unto them to this end, that men ought always to pray, and not to faint;...And shall not God avenge his own elect, which cry day and night unto him, though he bear

long with them? I tell you that he will avenge them speedily. Nevertheless when the Son of man cometh, shall he find faith on the earth?" Luke 18:1, 7, 8

iii) **Focus your mind on eternal realities not on distressing circumstances.**

"While we look not at the things which are seen, but at the things which are not seen: for the things which are seen are temporal; but the things which are not seen are eternal." 2 Cor 4:18

---

4 The Love of God is the Weapon Against Fear

Fear is the motivation which drives the negative thinking in satanic strongholds.

It may be fear that you will lose your popularity; fear that you may not be accepted by your peer group; fear of being forsaken by family or friends; fear that someone else may be more successful than you; fear that God has not forgiven you; fear of difficulties, and the ultimate fear—the fear of death or of being lost. The good news is that the love of God expels fear from the soul.

"And we have known and believed the love that God hath to us. God is love; and he that dwelleth in love dwelleth in God, and God in him. Herein is our love made perfect, that we may have boldness in the day of judgment: because as he is, so are we in this world. There is no fear in love; but perfect love casteth out fear: because fear hath torment. He that feareth is not made perfect in love. We love him, because he first loved us." 1 John 4:16-19

"Forasmuch then as the children are partakers of flesh and blood, he also himself likewise took part of the same; that through death he might destroy him that had the power of death, that is, the devil; And deliver them who through fear of death were all their lifetime subject to bondage." Hebrews 2:14,15

"These things I have spoken unto you, that in me ye might have peace. In the world ye shall have tribulation: but be of good cheer; I have overcome the world." John 16:33

"All that the Father giveth me shall come to me; and him that cometh to me I will in no wise cast out...Verily, verily, I say unto you, He that believeth on me hath everlasting life." John 6:37,47

5
Adversity is Used By God to Uncover Our Hidden Defects

God allows difficulty, trial, provocation, interpersonal friction, church problems, family life challenges etc., to show us what defects are hidden deep down.

"My brethren, count it all joy when ye fall into divers temptations; Knowing this, that the trying of your faith worketh patience. But let patience have her perfect work, that ye may be perfect and entire, wanting nothing." James 1:2-4

"Therefore being justified by faith, we have peace with God through our Lord Jesus Christ: By whom also we have access by faith into this grace wherein we stand, and rejoice in hope of the glory of God. And not only so, but we glory in tribulations also: knowing that tribulation worketh patience; And patience, experience; and experience, hope: And hope maketh not ashamed; because the love of God is shed abroad in our hearts by the Holy Ghost which is given unto us." Romans 5:1-5

"Who are kept by the power of God through faith unto salvation ready to be revealed in the last time. Wherein ye greatly rejoice, though now for a season, if need be, ye are in heaviness through manifold temptations: That the trial of your faith, being much more precious than of gold that perisheth, though it be tried with fire, might be found unto praise and honour and glory at the appearing of Jesus Christ: Whom having not seen, ye love; in whom, though now ye see him not, yet believing, ye rejoice with joy unspeakable and full of glory: Receiving the end of your faith, even the salvation of your souls." 1 Peter 1:5-9

"And we know that all things work together for good to them that love God, to them who are the called according to his purpose." Romans 8:28

Victorious Mind-Sets

When a defective mind-set, a satanic stronghold, is conquered it is replaced by a victory circuit. In contrast to a satanic stronghold, a victory circuit or divine stronghold has the following characteristics:

1. It is **Christ-Centred**
2. It is built upon **doctrinal truth** and the **behavioural truth** of God's character as revealed in Christ.
3. It is **positive** in direction, i.e. it is in harmony with the **positive principles** of the **self-sacrificing Agape love** of God
4. It is motivated by love and not by fear.
5. It is built deep and solidly into the mind by the Holy Spirit.
6. Under provocation it produces Christ-like behaviour.
7. It produces rest.

Here now is the diagram of a victory circuit:

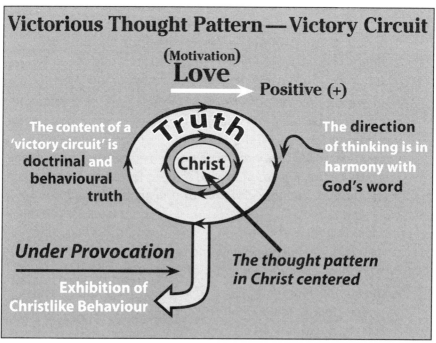

Diagram of a Victory Circuit

Practical Points

Paul advises us to examine ourselves. This is done through earnest prayer and study of the word of God and uncompromising evaluation of our behaviour (motives, thoughts, words, actions and reactions) while fixing our minds on Christ!

Welcome challenges, rejoice in adversity. Let the Holy Spirit uncover and bring to your awareness your deepseated defects so that you may repent and give up the defect and have it replaced with the corresponding attribute of the character of Christ.

Remember that a pessimist sees difficulties in every opportunity whereas an optimist sees opportunities in every difficulty!

"Our sorrows do not spring out of the ground. God "doth not afflict willingly nor grieve the children of men." Lamentations 3:33. When He permits trials and afflictions, it is "for our profit, that we might be partakers of His holiness." Hebrews 12:10. If received in faith, the trial that seems so bitter and hard to bear will prove a blessing. The cruel blow that blights the joys of earth will be the means of turning our eyes to heaven. How many there are who would never have known Jesus had not sorrow led them to seek comfort in Him!

"The trials of life are God's workmen, to remove the impurities and roughness from our character. Their hewing, squaring, and chiseling, their burnishing and polishing, is a painful process; it is hard to be pressed down to the grinding wheel. But the stone is brought forth prepared to fill its place in the heavenly temple. Upon no useless material does the Master bestow such careful, thorough work. Only His precious stones are polished after the similitude of a palace." MB 10

Omnipotent Power Available

"Henceforward Christ's followers were to look upon Satan as a conquered foe. Upon the cross, Jesus was to gain the victory for them; that victory He desired them to accept as their own. "Behold," He said, "I give unto you power to tread on serpents and scorpions, and over all the power of the enemy: and nothing shall by any means hurt you."

"The omnipotent power of the Holy Spirit is the defense of every contrite soul. Not one that in penitence and faith has claimed His protection will Christ permit to pass under the enemy's power. The Saviour is by the side of His tempted and tried ones. **With Him there can be no such thing as failure, loss, impossibility, or defeat; we can do all things through Him who strengthens us. When temptations and trials come, do not wait to adjust all the difficulties, but look to Jesus, your helper.**

"There are Christians who think and speak altogether too much about the power of Satan. They think of their adversary, they pray about him, they talk about him, and he looms up greater and greater in their imagination. It is true that Satan is a powerful being; but, thank God, we have a mighty Saviour, who cast out the evil one from heaven. Satan is pleased when we magnify his power. Why not talk of Jesus? Why not magnify His power and His love?

"The rainbow of promise encircling the throne on high is an everlasting testimony that "God so loved the world, that He gave His only-begotten Son, that whosoever believeth in Him should not perish, but have everlasting life." John 3:16. It testifies to the universe that God will never forsake His people in their struggle with evil. It is an assurance to us of strength and protection as long as the throne itself shall endure.

"Jesus added, "Notwithstanding in this rejoice not, that the spirits are subject unto you; but rather rejoice, because your names are written in heaven." Rejoice not in the possession of power, lest you lose sight of your dependence upon God. Be careful lest self-sufficiency come in, and you work in your own strength, rather than in the spirit and strength of your Master. Self is ever ready to take the credit if any measure of success attends the work. Self is flattered and exalted, and the impression is not made upon other minds that God is all and in all. The apostle Paul says, "When I am weak, then am I strong." 2 Cor. 12:10. When we have a realization of our weakness, we learn to depend upon a power not inherent. Nothing can take so strong a hold on the heart as the abiding sense of our responsibility to God. **Nothing reaches so fully down to the deepest motives of conduct as a sense of the pardoning love of Christ.** We are to come in touch with God, then we shall be imbued with His Holy Spirit, that enables us to come in touch with our fellow men. Then rejoice that through Christ you have become connected with God, members of the heavenly family. While you look higher than yourself, you will have a continual sense of the weakness of humanity. The less you cherish self, the more distinct and full will be your comprehension of the excellence of your Saviour. The more closely you connect yourself with the source of light and power, the greater light will be shed upon you, and the greater power will be yours to work for God. Rejoice that you are one with God, one with Christ, and with the whole family of heaven." DA 490

Appeal and Challenge

"Life is disciplinary. While in the world, the Christian will meet with adverse influences. **There will be provocations to test the temper; and it is by meeting these in a right spirit that the Christian graces are developed. If injuries and insults are meekly borne, if insulting words are responded to by gentle answers, and oppressive acts by kindness, this is evidence that the Spirit of Christ dwells in the heart, that sap from the living Vine is flowing to the branches.** We are in the school of Christ in this life, where we are to learn to be meek and lowly of heart; and in the day of final accounts we shall see that all the obstacles we meet, all the hardships and annoyances that we are called to bear, are practical lessons in the application of principles of Christian life. If well endured, they develop the Christlike in the character and distinguish the Christian from the worldling." 5T 344

Always remember that we are more than conquerors through the victorious love of God in Christ.

"Who shall separate us from the love of Christ? shall tribulation, or distress, or persecution, or famine, or nakedness, or peril, or sword? As it is written, For thy sake we are killed all the day long; we are accounted as sheep for the slaughter. Nay, in all these things we are more than conquerors through him that loved us. For I am persuaded, that neither death, nor life, nor angels, nor principalities, nor powers, nor things present, nor things to come, Nor height, nor depth, nor any other creature, shall be able to separate us from the love of God, which is in Christ Jesus our Lord." Romans 8:35-39.

15 The Victorious Power of the Gospel

In Chapter 11 we studied A.T. Jones explaining that God sets up His kingdom in the innermost recesses of the mind, the seat or fountain of the thoughts. Modern neurophysiology has shown that there is a mysterious area deep down in the central base of the brain which is responsible for "emotional intelligence" and "reflex" outbursts of certain behavioural traits. This part of the brain is called the **limbic system.**

In 1975 Harvard physician Dr Herbert Benson demonstrated that a certain part of the limbic system called the **amygdala** showed greatest electrical activity during religious exercises. This led neuroscientist Shwan Joseph to conclude that the ability to have religious experiences has a neuro-anatomical basis. Our brains were made with the ability to **respond** to God's love!

As our kidneys are programmed to excrete wastes and our intestines to digest and absorb nutrients, so our brains are "wired" to praise God. When we praise God the electrical impulses of the brain stimulate the production of positive chemical endorphins which enhance mental and physical health!

> *"This people have I formed for myself; they shall shew forth my praise." Isaiah 43:21*

"Why art thou cast down, O my soul? and why art thou disquieted within me? hope thou in God: for I shall yet praise him, who is the health of my countenance, and my God." Psalm 42:11

"Nothing tends more to promote health of body and of soul than does a spirit of gratitude and praise. **It is a positive duty to resist melancholy, discontented thoughts and feelings - as much a duty as it is to pray.** If we are heaven-bound, how can we go as a band of mourners, groaning and complaining all along the way to our Father's house?

"Those professed Christians who are constantly complaining, and who seem to think cheerfulness and happiness a sin, have not genuine religion. Those who take a mournful pleasure in all that is melancholy in the natural world, who choose to look upon dead leaves rather than to gather the beautiful living flowers, who see no beauty in grand mountain heights and in valleys clothed with living green, who close their senses to the joyful voice which speaks to them in nature, and which is sweet and musical to the listening ear—these are not in Christ. They are gathering to themselves gloom and darkness, when they might have brightness, even the Sun of Righteousness arising in their hearts with healing in His beams.

"Often your mind may be clouded because of pain. Then do not try to think. You know that Jesus loves you. He understands your weakness. You may do His will by simply resting in His arms.

"It is a law of nature that our thoughts and feelings are encouraged and strengthened as we give them utterance. While words express thoughts, it is also true that thoughts follow words. If we would give more expression to our faith, rejoice more in the blessings that we know we have,—the great mercy and love of God,—we should have more faith and greater joy. No tongue can express, no finite mind can conceive, the blessing that results from appreciating the goodness and love of God. Even on earth we may have joy as a wellspring, never failing, because we are fed by the streams that flow from the throne of God.

"Then let us educate our hearts and lips to speak the praise of God for His matchless love. Let us educate our souls to be hopeful and to abide in the light shining from the cross of Calvary. Never should we forget that we are children of the heavenly King, sons and daughters of the Lord of hosts. It is our privilege to maintain a calm repose in God.

"Let the peace of God rule in your hearts; . . . and be ye thankful." Colossians 3:15. Forgetting our own difficulties and troubles, let us praise God for an opportunity to live for the glory of His name. Let the fresh blessings of each new day awaken praise in our hearts for these tokens of His loving care. When you open your eyes in the morning, thank God that He has kept you through the night. Thank Him for His peace in your heart. Morning, noon, and night, let gratitude as a sweet perfume ascend to heaven.

"When someone asks how you are feeling, do not try to think of something mournful to tell in order to gain sympathy. Do not talk of your lack of faith and your sorrows and sufferings. The tempter delights to hear such words. When talking on gloomy subjects, you are glorifying him. We are not to dwell on the great power of Satan to overcome us. Often we give ourselves into his hands by talking of his power. Let us talk instead of the great power of God to bind up all our interests with His own. Tell of the matchless power of Christ, and speak of His glory. All heaven is interested in our salvation. The angels of God, thousands upon thousands, and ten thousand times ten thousand, are commissioned to minister to those who shall be heirs of salvation. They guard us against evil and press back the powers of darkness that are seeking our destruction. Have we not reason to be thankful every moment, thankful even when there are apparent difficulties in our pathway? MH 251

Discouragement destroys hope and that is why Satan always tries to discourage us. Without hope we give up, which is what the devil wants us to do. But the scriptures repeatedly tell us not to be discouraged or dismayed.

> *"Fear thou not; for I am with thee: be not dismayed; for I am thy God: I will strengthen thee; yea, I will help thee; yea, I will uphold thee with the right hand of my righteousness."* Isaiah 41:10

> *"These things I have spoken unto you, that in me ye might have peace. In the world ye shall have tribulation: but be of good cheer; I have overcome the world."* John 16:33

The limbic system is the store-house of cultivated defects which trigger the kind of behaviour we call **"flying off the handle."** Psychologists call it the **"amygdala-reflex."**

But, as we have seen before, the study of God's character as revealed in the life and death of His Son and the surrender of the **will-power, intellect** and **emotions** to God's love, will re-program the amygdala to produce righteous behaviour even under adversity!

In the process of sanctification unto perfection of character, God, in Christ by the Holy Spirit, will completely renew our minds by removing all deep-seated, cultivated defects of character and build in the beautiful attributes of Agapé Christ-like character.

Cleansing out doctrinal error and implanting doctrinal truth involve especially the frontal lobes and the parietal lobes, the intellectual centers, of the brain. Whereas cleansing out behavioural error and building in right behaviour involve especially the **limbic system** and the **amygdala**.

Furthermore, whereas the change from doctrinal error to doctrinal truth requires logical persuasion based upon the principles of Bible truth; the change from wrong to right behaviour requires beholding the life of Christ and the motivation of the love of God!

The True Gospel Of The Jones-Waggoner Message And Victory Over Defects

When Adam sold out the human race by his one act of disobedience there was created a void of insecurity and rejection in the human spirit, a hopeless emptiness.

There is nothing other than the true gospel to satisfy this deep longing in the human soul for security and acceptance and love!

The true gospel proclaims the wonderful news that the eternal Son of God became truly human and took on our **fallen** human nature. In Him divinity and humanity were united in such a mysterious blend that He had an undivided personality. He entered into our human experiences, was really tempted in all points like as we are. He overcame all temptation by faith which surrendered fully to His Father's will. He therefore lived a sinless life in our **sinful** flesh which He took on. He condemned sin in the flesh. Throughout His entire life He was engaged in the terrible lifelong conflict with "self" because He took on our fallen human nature.

But not only that, He actually bore the full weight of all the guilt and shame and damage which sin has done to the human mind. He perfectly obeyed God's law for Adam's lost race and He died the second death for all men.

By His perfect obedience and infinite sacrifice on the cross He paid the redemption price for all mankind, i.e. every single human being who has ever lived or who will ever live! He suffered and exhausted the punishment for all sin of all mankind.

This brings us now to the fantastically wonderful news. Corporate humanity, all men, were legally bought back or legally redeemed by Christ's sacrifice. God has credited to every human being the full benefits of the sacrifice of Christ. Therefore, for **all** humanity, the condemnation to eternal death caused by Adam's disobedience was legally abolished by Christ's sacrifice. He was and is truly the Saviour of **all** men, of the **whole** world. In Christ, God has actually given to all men the gift of salvation. All men are legally redeemed!

But God will force no one to accept the free gift. Those who genuinely **believe** and receive the free gift are saved. Those who **reject** the free gift, who will not give to Jesus their souls that He has **already** purchased, will be lost.

Moreover, because He was **not** exempt from our fallen heredity, Jesus knows by experience the **terrible pull** of the sinful flesh on the mind. He never cherished any tempting thought. He never allowed the pull of the flesh to form character defects in His soul. Therefore He knows how to **"succour" us, how to "nurse"** us in and through the process of obtaining the victory over temptation and over any and all defects, hereditary and cultivated. And we have already studied A.T. Jones on that subject in Chapters 10, 11, 12!

This wonderful love of God, revealed in what He has already done for us and given to us in Christ, is the **goodness** of God that produces genuine repentance in the soul and enables us to confess and surrender fully to God to allow His Spirit to set up His kingdom in the spirit of our minds and to reign until our characters are perfected! Consider carefully the following texts and quotations:

> *"There is also no comparison between God's gift and the one who sinned. The verdict which followed one person's failure condemned everyone. But, even after many failures, the gift brought God's approval...Therefore, everyone was condemned through one failure, and everyone received God's life-giving approval through one verdict." Romans 5: 16, 18 (GW)*

> *"For the love of Christ constraineth us; because we thus judge, that if one died for all, then were all dead:...And all things are of God, who hath reconciled us to himself by Jesus Christ, and hath given to us the ministry of reconciliation; To wit, that God was in Christ, reconciling the world unto himself, not imputing their trespasses unto them; and hath committed unto us the word of reconciliation. Now then we are ambassadors for Christ, as though God did beseech you by us: we pray you in Christ's stead, be ye reconciled to God." 2 Cor 5:14,18,19,20*

> *"And we have seen and do testify that the Father sent the Son to be the Saviour of the world." 1 John 4:14*

> *"But we see Jesus, who was made a little lower than the angels for the suffering of death, crowned with glory and honour; that he by the grace of God should taste death for every man." Hebrew 2:9*

> *"Seeing then that we have a great high priest, that is passed into the heavens, Jesus the Son of God, let us hold fast our profession. For we have not an high priest which cannot be touched with the feeling of our infirmities; but was in*

*all points tempted like as we are, yet without sin. Let us therefore come boldly unto the throne of grace, that we may obtain mercy, and find grace to help in time of need."
Hebrews 4:14-16*

"Forasmuch then as the children are partakers of flesh and blood, he also himself likewise took part of the same; that through death he might destroy him that had the power of death, that is, the devil; And deliver them who through fear of death were all their lifetime subject to bondage. For verily he took not on him the nature of angels; but he took on him the seed of Abraham. Wherefore in all things it behoved him to be made like unto his brethren, that he might be a merciful and faithful high priest in things pertaining to God, to make reconciliation for the sins of the people. For in that he himself hath suffered being tempted, he is able to succour them that are tempted." Heb 2:14-18

"Justice demands that sin be not merely pardoned, but the death penalty must be executed. God, in the gift of His only-begotten Son, met both these requirements. By dying in man's stead, Christ exhausted the penalty and provided a pardon.

"Man through sin has been severed from the life of God. His soul is palsied through the machinations of Satan, the author of sin. Of himself he is incapable of sensing sin, incapable of appreciating and appropriating the divine nature. Were it brought within his reach, there is nothing in it that his natural heart would desire it. The bewitching power of Satan is upon him. All the ingenious subterfuges the devil can suggest are presented to his mind to prevent every good impulse. Every faculty and power given him of God has been used as a weapon against the divine Benefactor. So, although He loves him, God cannot safely impart to him the gifts and blessings He desires to bestow.

"But God will not be defeated by Satan. He sent His Son into the world, that through His taking the human form and nature, humanity and divinity combined in Him would elevate man in the scale of moral value with God.

"There is no other way for man's salvation. "Without me," says Christ, "ye can do nothing" (John 15:5). Through Christ, and Christ alone, the springs of life can vitalize man's nature, transform his tastes, and set his affections flowing toward heaven. Through the union of the divine with the human nature, Christ could enlighten the understanding and infuse His life-giving properties through the soul dead in trespasses and sins.

"When the mind is drawn to the cross of Calvary, Christ by imperfect sight is discerned on the shameful cross. Why did He die? In consequence of sin. What is sin? The transgression of the law. Then the eyes are open to see the character of sin. The law is broken but cannot pardon the transgressor. It is our schoolmaster, condemning to punishment. Where is the remedy? The law drives us to Christ, who was hanged upon the cross that He might be able to impart His righteousness to fallen, sinful man and thus present men to His Father in His righteous character.

"Christ on the cross not only draws men to repentance toward God for the transgression of His law--for whom God pardons He first makes penitent--but Christ has satisfied Justice; He has proffered Himself as an atonement. His gushing blood, His broken body, satisfy the claims of the broken law, and thus He bridges the gulf which sin has made. He suffered in the flesh, that with His bruised and broken body He might cover the defenseless sinner. The victory gained at His death on Calvary broke forever the accusing power of Satan over the universe and silenced his charges that self-denial was impossible with God and therefore not essential in the human family.

"Satan's position in heaven had been next to the Son of God. He was first among the angels. His power had been debasing, but God could not reveal it in its true light and carry all heaven in harmony with Him in removing him with his evil influences. His power was increasing, but the evil was yet unrecognized. It was a deadly power to the universe, but for the security of the worlds and the government of heaven, it was necessary that it should develop and be revealed in its true light.

"In carrying out his enmity to Christ until He hung upon the cross of Calvary, with wounded, bruised body and broken heart, Satan completely uprooted himself from the affections of the universe. It was then seen that God had in His Son denied Himself, giving Himself for the sins of the world, because He loved mankind. The Creator was revealed in the Son of the infinite God. Here the question, "Can there be self-denial with God?" was forever answered. Christ was God, and condescending to be made flesh, He assumed humanity and became obedient unto death, that He might undergo infinite sacrifice.

"Whatever sacrifice a human being could undergo Christ endured, notwithstanding Satan put forth every effort to seduce Him with temptations; but the greater the temptation, the more perfect was the sacrifice. All that was possible for man to endure in the conflict with Satan, Christ endured in His human and divine nature combined. Obedient, sinless to the last, He died for man, his substitute and surety, enduring all that men ever endure from the deceiving tempter, that man may overcome by being a partaker of the divine nature.

"Pure truth was found to be a match for falsehood, honesty and integrity for subtlety and intrigue, in everyone who is, like Christ, willing to sacrifice all, even life itself, for the truth's sake. To resist Satan's desires is no easy task. It demands a firm hold of the divine nature from beginning to end, or it cannot be done. Christ, in the victories achieved in His death on Calvary's cross, plainly lays open the way for man, and thus makes it possible for him to keep the law of God through the Way, the Truth, and the Life. There is no other way.

"The righteousness of Christ is presented as a free gift to the sinner if he will accept it. He has nothing of his own but what is tainted and corrupted, polluted with sin, utterly repulsive to a pure and holy God. Only through the righteous character of Jesus Christ can man come nigh to God.

"Christ as high priest within the veil so immortalized Calvary that though He liveth unto God, He dies continually to sin, and thus if any man sin, he has an advocate with the Father.

"He arose from the tomb enshrouded with a cloud of angels in wondrous power and glory--the Deity and humanity combined. **He took in His grasp the world over which Satan claimed to preside as his lawful territory, and by His wonderful work in giving His life, He restored the whole race of men to favor with God. . . .**

"**Let no one take the limited, narrow position that any of the works of man can help in the least possible way to liquidate the debt of his transgression. This is a fatal deception. If you would understand it, you must cease haggling over your pet ideas, and with humble hearts survey the atonement. This matter is so dimly comprehended that thousands upon thousands claiming to be sons of God are children of the wicked one, because they will depend on their own works. God always demanded good works, the law demands it, but because man placed himself in sin where his good works were valueless, Jesus' righteousness alone can avail. Christ is able to save to the uttermost because He ever liveth to make intercession for us. All that man can possibly do toward his own salvation is to accept the invitation, "Whosoever will, let him take the water of life freely" (Rev. 22:17). No sin can be committed by man for which satisfaction has not been met on Calvary. Thus the cross, in earnest appeals, continually proffers to the sinner a thorough expiation.**

"As you near the cross of Calvary there is seen love that is without a parallel. As you by faith grasp the meaning of the sacrifice, you see yourself a sinner, condemned by a broken law. This is repentance. As you come with humble heart, you find pardon, for Christ Jesus is represented as continually standing at the altar, momentarily offering up the sacrifice for the sins of the world. He is a minister of the true tabernacle which the Lord pitched and not man. The typical shadows of the Jewish tabernacle no longer possess any virtue. A daily and yearly typical atonement is no longer to be made, but the atoning sacrifice through a mediator is essential because of the constant commission of sin. Jesus is officiating in the presence of God, offering up His shed blood, as it had been a lamb slain. Jesus presents the oblation offered for every offense and every shortcoming of the sinner.

"Christ, our Mediator, and the Holy Spirit are constantly interceding in man's behalf, but the Spirit pleads not for us as does Christ, who presents His blood, shed from the foundation of the world; the Spirit works upon our hearts, drawing out prayers and penitence, praise and thanksgiving. The gratitude which flows from our lips is the result of the Spirit's striking the cords of the soul in holy memories, awakening the music of the heart.

"The religious services, the prayers, the praise, the penitent confession of sin ascend from true believers as incense to the heavenly sanctuary, but passing through the corrupt channels of humanity, they are so defiled that unless purified by blood, they can never be of value with God. They ascend not in spotless purity, and unless the Intercessor, who is at God's right hand, presents and purifies all by His righteousness, it is not acceptable to God. All incense from earthly tabernacles must be moist with the cleansing drops of the blood of Christ. He holds before the Father the censer of His own merits, in which there is no taint of earthly corruption. He gathers into this censer the prayers, the praise, and the confessions of His people, and with these He puts His own spotless righteousness. Then, perfumed with the merits of Christ's propitiation, the incense comes up before God wholly and entirely acceptable. Then gracious answers are returned.

"Oh, that all may see that everything in obedience, in penitence, in praise and thanksgiving, must be placed upon the glowing fire of the righteousness of Christ. The fragrance of this righteousness ascends like a cloud around the mercy seat." (Manuscript 50, 1900) 1SM 340-344

"Repentance, as well as forgiveness, is the gift of God through Christ. It is through the influence of the Holy Spirit that we are convicted of sin, and feel our need of pardon. None but the contrite are forgiven; but it is the grace of God that makes the heart penitent. He is acquainted with all our weaknesses and infirmities, and He will help us.

"Some who come to God by repentance and confession, and even believe that their sins are forgiven, still fail of claiming, as they should, the promises of God. They do not see that Jesus is an ever-present Saviour; and they are not ready to commit the keeping of their souls to Him, relying upon Him to perfect the work of grace begun in their hearts. While they think they are committing themselves to God, there is a great deal of self-dependence. There are conscientious souls that trust partly to God, and partly to themselves. They do not look to God, to be kept by His power, but depend upon watchfulness against temptation, and the performance of certain duties for acceptance with Him. There are no victories in this kind of faith. Such persons toil to no purpose; their souls are in continual bondage, and they find no rest until their burdens are laid at the feet of Jesus.

"There is need of constant watchfulness, and of earnest, loving devotion; but these will come naturally when the soul is kept by the power of God through faith. We can do nothing, absolutely nothing, to commend ourselves to divine favor. We must not trust at all to ourselves nor to our good works; but when as erring, sinful beings we come to Christ, we may find rest in His love. God will accept every one that comes to Him trusting wholly in the merits of a crucified Saviour. Love springs up in the heart. There may be no ecstasy of feeling, but there is an abiding, peaceful trust. Every burden is light; for the yoke which Christ imposes is easy. Duty becomes a delight, and sacrifice a pleasure. The path that before seemed shrouded in darkness becomes bright with beams from the Sun of Righteousness. This is walking in the light as Christ is in the light." 1SM 353, 354

All men have been bought with this infinite price. By pouring the whole treasury of heaven into this world, by giving us in Christ all heaven, God has purchased the will, the affections, the mind, the soul, of every human being. Whether believers or unbelievers, all men are the Lord's property. All are called to do service for Him, and for the manner in which they have met this claim, all will be required to render an account at the great judgment day." COL 326

Jesus knows the circumstances of every soul. The greater the sinner's guilt, the more he needs the Saviour. His heart of divine love and sympathy is drawn out most of all for the one who is the most hopelessly entangled in the snares of the enemy. **With His own blood He has signed the emancipation papers of the race".** MH 89

16 Something Has Gone Terribly Wrong...

Our great High Priest Jesus Christ entered the Most Holy Place of the Heavenly Sanctuary on October 22, 1844. Ever since that time He has been waiting for *"His wife to make herself ready"* (Revelation 19:7)

Four generations have passed since then. We must conclude, and correctly so, that something has gone terribly wrong.

We have already seen that Laodicean lukewarmness developed quite early in the first generation (1844-1884). The lukewarm condition continued its malignant growth despite a multiplicity of warnings sent by God through Sis E.G. White.

We have also examined the fact that early in the second generation, 1888 to be exact, God intervened in a most emphatic way. He sent the wonderful message of the covenants and righteousness by faith through Elders E.J. Waggoner and A.T. Jones.

By numerous endorsements (over 300) Sis White made plain the fact that the Jones-Waggoner messages on the covenants and righteousness by faith was the true light. In fact it was the beginning of what we Adventists call the "loud cry" by which we mean the final warning under the "latter rain" power of the Holy Spirit.

"The Lord in His great mercy sent a most precious message to His people through Elders Waggoner and Jones. This message was to bring more prominently before the world the uplifted Saviour, the sacrifice for the sins of the whole world. It presented justification through faith in the Surety; it invited the people to receive the righteousness of Christ, which is made manifest in obedience to all the commandments of God. Many had lost sight of Jesus. They needed to have their eyes directed to His divine person, His merits, and His changeless love for the human family. All power is given into His hands, that He may dispense rich gifts unto men, imparting the priceless gift of His own righteousness to the helpless human agent. This is the message that God commanded to be given to the world. It is the third angel's message, which is to be proclaimed with a loud voice, and attended with the outpouring of His Spirit in a large measure." TM 91, 92

"Unless he makes it his life business to behold the uplifted Saviour, and by faith to accept the merits which it is his privilege to claim, the sinner can no more be saved than Peter could walk upon the water unless he kept his eyes fixed steadily upon Jesus. Now, it has been Satan's determined purpose to eclipse the view of Jesus and lead men to look to man, and trust to man, and be educated to expect help from man. For years the church has been looking to man and expecting much from man, but not looking to Jesus, in whom our hopes of eternal life are centered. Therefore God gave to His servants a testimony that presented the truth as it is in Jesus, which is the third angel's message, in clear, distinct lines." TM 93

"The time of test is just upon us, for the loud cry of the third angel has already begun in the revelation of the righteousness of Christ, the sin-pardoning Redeemer. This is the beginning of the light of the angel whose glory shall fill the whole earth." RH Nov 22, 1892

"The present message—justification by faith—is a message from God; it bears the divine credentials, for its fruit is unto holiness. Some who greatly need the precious truth that was presented before them, we fear, did not receive its benefit. They did not open the door of their hearts to welcome Jesus as a heavenly guest, and they have suffered great loss. There is indeed a narrow way in which we must walk; the cross is presented at every step. We must learn to live by faith; then the darkest hours will be brightened by the blessed beams of the Sun of Righteousness." RH Sept 3, 1889

"The enemy of man and God is not willing that this truth should be clearly presented; for he knows that if the people receive it fully, his power will be broken. If he can control minds so that doubt and unbelief and darkness shall compose the experience of those who claim to be the children of God, he can overcome them with temptation. That simple faith that takes God at his word should be encouraged. God's people must have that faith which will lay hold of divine power; "for by grace are ye saved through faith; and that not of yourselves: it is the gift of God." Not all will receive the light, forsake their sins, and believe the words of eternal life, and without drawing back, go on from one truth to another, until guided into all truth. Those who believe that God for Christ's sake has forgiven their sins, should not, through temptation, fail to press on to fight the good fight of faith. Their faith should grow stronger until their Christian life, as well as their words, shall declare, "The blood of Jesus Christ cleanseth me from all sin." RH Sept 3, 1889

The Holy Spirit came down with latter rain blessings for the finishing of the work. Heaven intended to finish the work (which should have been finished in the first generation) early in the second generation.

So, the question is, what happened? Something terrible happened!

Whatever happened back there in 1888 (and the following 13 years) committed the Seventh Day Adventist Church to an embarrassingly lengthy "wilderness march" going around in circles but going no where near the "promised land."

So, the question still is, what happened?

The heaven-sent message on the covenants and righteousness by faith was rejected!

Heaven vibrated with the shock of disappointment!

Listen to Sis White:

> "The law was our schoolmaster to bring us unto Christ, that we might be justified by faith" (Gal. 3:24). In this scripture, the Holy Spirit through the apostle is speaking especially of the moral law. The law reveals sin to us, and causes us to feel our need of Christ and to flee unto Him for pardon and peace by exercising repentance toward God and faith toward our Lord Jesus Christ.

> "An unwillingness to yield up preconceived opinions, and to accept this truth, lay at the foundation of a large share of the opposition manifested at Minneapolis against the Lord's message through Brethren {E.J.} Waggoner and {A.T.} Jones. By exciting that opposition Satan succeeded in shutting away from our people, in a great measure, the special power of the Holy Spirit that God longed to impart to them. The enemy prevented them from obtaining that efficiency which might have been theirs in carrying the truth to the world, as the apostles proclaimed it after the day of Pentecost. The light that is to lighten the whole earth with its glory was resisted, and by the action of our own brethren has been in a great degree kept away from the world. 1SM 234, 235

And, selections from a letter she wrote from Australia in 1892:

> "The only hope for our churches today is to repent and do their first work....Well may the people fear and tremble under these words: 'Except thou repent, I will come unto thee quickly, and will remove thy candlestick out of his place.' What then? 'If therefore the light that is in thee be darkness, how great is that darkness!'... God's people have evidence piled upon evidence; they have truth powerful and convincing. Shall it be kept in the outer court ...? **Why do not brethren of like precious faith consider that in every age, when the Lord has sent a special message to the people, all the powers of the confederacy of**

evil have set at work to prevent the word of truth from coming to those who should receive it. Now, although there has been a determined effort to make of no effect the message God has sent, its fruits have been proving that it was from the source of light and truth. One matter burdens my soul: The great lack of the love God, which has been lost through continued resistance to light and truth ...in the face of evidence piled upon evidence, have exerted an influence to counteract the work of the message God has sent. I point them to the Jewish nation and ask, Must we leave our brethren to pass over the same path of blind resistance, till the very end of probation? ... What a condition of blindness. ... 'wretched, and miserable, and poor, and blind, and naked.' The guilt of self-deception is upon our churches. The religious life of many is a lie. ... Evidence has been piled upon evidence, but they have been unwilling to acknowledge it. ...The time will come when many will be willing to do anything and everything possible in order to have a chance of hearing the call which they rejected at Minneapolis. ... The sin committed in what took place at Minneapolis remains on the record books of heaven. ...When God speaks to men, commanding them to bear His message to the people, it means something ... Those who claim to know the truth, and yet lay every obstacle in the way so that light shall not come to the people, will have an account to settle with God that they will not be pleased to meet. God manages His own work, and woe to the man who puts his hand to the ark of God". (1888 Materials, pp. 1020-1032)

The second generation 1884-1924 ended without the harvest being ripened, without the "wife" being made ready.

As we have already seen the third generation 1924-1964 was one not only of compromise and apostasy but of continued rejection of the 1888 message.

In 1950 Pastors Robert Wieland and Donald Short presented a manuscript entitled *1888 Re-examined*. It was a call to (i) study and accept the 1888 message; (ii) express corporate denominational repentance for the sin of rejection in 1888 and (iii) to share the message with the world-wide membership.

Both the **manuscript** and the **call** were not only rejected but in fact, condemned! This official rejection occurred in 1958. But a number of church members received the manuscript and agitation or "shaking" began.

Since then some major books have been published with the blessings of the General Conference leadership, books which ignore, defy, or reject the E.G. White materials on what really happened in 1888. Here is a list:

1. 1962 *By Faith Alone* by Norval F. Pease
2. 1966 *Through Crisis to Victory 1888-1901* by A.V. Olsen
3. 1971 *Movement of Destiny* by LeRoy E. Froom
4. 1987 *From 1888 to Apostasy: The Case of A. T. Jones* by George R. Knight
5. 1989 *Angry Saints* by George R. Knight
6. 1994 *The Nature of Christ* by Roy Adams
7. 1998 *A User-friendly Guide to the 1888 Message* by George R. Knight.

All of these books misrepresent the true facts of the history of 1888. Roy Adams' book *The Nature of Christ* is an outright rejection of one of the central truths of the true gospel as presented in 1888, that Christ in the incarnation took on our fallen sinful flesh. George Knight in his books downgrades Jones and the message. Froom's book came with high recommendations by leaders and scholars. It presented 1888 as a victory for the truth. This was a denial of E.G. White's comments that the message was rejected.

In addition to these books which have sought to side step the issues, something else was done. New editions of certain books which are compilations of certain E.G. White writings contained **explanations** by compilers, **explanations** which are used to give a certain biased understanding of the 1888 message and history. For example the 33 page account of the Minneapolis Conference in *Selected Messages Book 3* and a 22 page Historical Foreword in the new edition of *Testimonies To Ministers.*

But scholars and compilers cannot change history. The true history of the 1888 Minneapolis General Conference Session stands written in heaven. The record of the Lord's messenger, Sis White, cannot be altered even by "cover up" or deception! Writing from Australia in 1869 Ellen White penned this solemn warning.

> "If men would only give up their spirit of resistance to the Holy Spirit, the spirit which has long been leaving their religious experience, God's Spirit would address itself to their hearts. It would convince of sin. What a work! But the Holy Spirit has been insulted and light has been rejected. Is it possible for those who for years have been so blind to see? Is it possible that in this late stage of their resistance their eyes will be anointed? Will the voice of the Spirit of God be distinguished from the deceiving voice of the enemy? 1888 Materials 1494

Moreover, she declared that all the universe witnessed the terrible rejection:

> "On many occasions the Holy Spirit did work, but those who resisted the Spirit of God at Minneapolis were waiting for a chance to travel over the same ground again, because their spirit was the same afterward, when they had evidence heaped upon evidence, some were convicted, but those who were not softened and subdued by the Holy Spirit's working, put their own interpretation upon every manifestation of the grace of God, and they have lost much. They pronounced in their heart and soul and words that this manifestation of the Holy Spirit was fanaticism and delusion. They stood like a rock, the waves of mercy flowing upon and around them, but beaten back by their hard and wicked hearts, which resisted the Holy Spirit's working. Had this been received, it would have made them wise unto salvation; holier men, prepared to do the work of God with sanctified ability. **But all the universe of heaven witnessed the disgraceful treatment of Jesus Christ, represented by the Holy Spirit. Had Christ been before them, they would have treated him in a manner similar to that in which the Jews treated Christ.** 1888 Materials 1478, 1479

Laodicean Blindness

The ecclesiastical authorities in Christ's day **could not see** that He was the true Messiah. Study John 9 and see how stubbornly blind they were. They rejected **evidence piled upon evidence** that Jesus was the Messiah. Listen to what Jesus told them.

> *"And some of the Pharisees which were with him heard these words, and said unto him, Are we blind also? Jesus said unto them, If ye were blind, ye should have no sin: but now ye say, We see; therefore your sin remaineth." John 9:40, 41*

Similarly there is an official spiritual blindness in Laodicea. Jesus the True and Faithful witness declares:

> "I know you inside and out, and find little to my liking. You're not cold, you're not hot – far better to be either cold or hot! You're stagnant. You make me want to vomit. You brag, "I'm rich, I've got it made, I need nothing from anyone,' oblivious that in fact you're a pitiful, blind beggar, threadbare and homeless."Here's what I want you to do: Buy your gold from Me, gold that's been through the refiner's fire. Then you'll be rich. Buy your clothes from Me, clothes designed in heaven. You've gone around half-naked long enough. And buy medicine for your eyes from Me so you can see, really see." Revelation 3:15-18 *The Message* (Eugene Peterson version).

Fourth Generation: Material Prosperity And Deepening Lukewarmness

The statistics of the church continue to show increasing prosperity, worldwide satellite evangelism, more members, more schools, more hospitals, more money, more degrees, more of everything that the world uses to measure success and progress. But these things have not finished the work nor can they do so. The work which could have been finished in the first or second generation is still unfinished after 4 generations!

The Adventist world continues to experience the **agitation** and **shaking** which results from the **conflict** between **true** Adventism and **false** Adventism! Indeed the iniquities of the fathers has been visited upon the **third** and **fourth** generations (Exodus 20:5)

Meanwhile Christ Is Waiting For And Preparing His Bride

Jesus Christ our High Priest, by His Spirit, has been and is working on hearts to accept the precious 1888 message and its advancing beams of light. More and more Adventists are being exposed to the tremendous truths of the 1888 message and the character of God. Some have been forced to teach and preach their truths outside of the "mainstream" organization. They are in good company, Christ had a similar experience.

> "The Sanhedrin had rejected Christ's message and was bent upon His death; therefore Jesus departed from Jerusalem, from the priests, the temple, the religious leaders, the people who had been instructed in the law, and turned to another class to proclaim His message, and to gather out those who should carry the gospel to all nations.

> "As the light and life of men was rejected by the ecclesiastical authorities in the days of Christ, so it has been rejected in every succeeding generation. Again and again the history of Christ's withdrawal from Judea has been repeated. When the Reformers preached the word of God, they had no thought of separating themselves from the established church; but the religious leaders would not tolerate the light, and those that bore it were forced to seek another class, who were longing for the truth. In our day few of the professed followers of the Reformers are actuated by their spirit. Few are listening for the voice of God, and ready to accept truth in whatever guise it may be presented. **Often those who follow in the steps of the Reformers are forced to turn away from the churches they love, in order to declare the plain teaching of the word of God. And many times those who are seeking for light are by the same teaching obliged to leave the church of their fathers, that they may render obedience. DA 232**

The true church is not defined by ecclesiastical lineage or by central offices or buildings but by being in Christ and His truth!

"The Pharisees had declared themselves the children of Abraham. Jesus told them that this claim could be established only by doing the works of Abraham. The true children of Abraham would live, as he did, a life of obedience to God. They would not try to kill One who was speaking the truth that was given Him from God. In plotting against Christ, the rabbis were not doing the works of Abraham. A mere lineal descent from Abraham was of no value. Without a spiritual connection with him, which would be manifested in possessing the same spirit, and doing the same works, they were not his children.

"This principle bears with equal weight upon a question that has long agitated the Christian world,–the question of apostolic succession. Descent from Abraham was proved, not by name and lineage, but by likeness of character. So the apostolic succession rests not upon the transmission of ecclesiastical authority, but upon spiritual relationship. A life actuated by the apostles' spirit, the belief and teaching of the truth they taught, this is the true evidence of apostolic succession. This is what constitutes men the successors of the first teachers of the gospel." DA 466-467

Official Rejection Of Light At The End Of The Fourth Generation

On May 12, 1994 the General Conference set in motion a PRIMACY OF THE GOSPEL *ad hoc* committee with a unique mandate:

> **"There is no prepared agenda, and the purpose of the meeting is to attempt to identify the causes of the apparent rift between the church and those focusing on 1888, and work at ways to heal the gap and bring a sense of unity."**

Over the 5 year period, 1994-1999, there were nine meetings, spread over sixteen and a half days, between the General Conference *ad hoc* committee and the 1888 Message Study Committee. Areas of agreement were noted, areas of disagreement were carefully studied.

The *ad hoc* General Conference committee maintained the earlier positions of the church leadership. There was no acceptance of the key Jones-Waggoner emphases on the human nature of Christ in the incarnation or legal redemption of humanity. Furthermore the General Conference Committee concluded by saying:

> "Therefore, we firmly believe that 1888 Study Committee should discontinue its claims that the true message of righteousness by faith was rejected by the leaders of the church, that they never genuinely accepted it, and that they have intentionally kept it away from the church and the world." PRIMACY OF THE GOSPEL COMMITTEE REPORT. February 2000.

So the official rejection of the 1888 message which took place in the second generation has continued on through the third and fourth generations. Where does that leave individual Seventh Day Adventist members?

Individual Responsibility

Each individual Adventist must now take responsibility for his or her salvation and not commit that responsibility to church leadership. Each member who intends to be harvest-ripe should study the 1888 message, believe and experience the true gospel with the advancing light of the message on God's character and allow the Holy Spirit to eradicate deep-seated defects from the character.

Moreover, we must repent for the sin of the 1888 message rejection and earnestly seek the Lord with all our hearts, in true repentance and humility, praying for the latter rain and walking in the light. We must pray for the worldwide church that God will indeed bring every honest soul to "see" the light and be prepared for the end.

In Ellen White's vision of the "Shaking" she saw two groups. Which group will you be in?

> "I saw some, with strong faith and agonizing cries, pleading with God. Their countenances were pale and marked with deep anxiety, expressive of their internal struggle. Firmness and great earnestness was expressed in their countenances; large drops of perspiration fell from their foreheads. Now

and then their faces would light up with the marks of God's approbation, and again the same solemn, earnest, anxious look would settle upon them.

"Evil angels crowded around, pressing darkness upon them to shut out Jesus from their view, that their eyes might be drawn to the darkness that surrounded them, and thus they be led to distrust God and murmur against Him. Their only safety was in keeping their eyes directed upward. Angels of God had charge over His people, and as the poisonous atmosphere of evil angels was pressed around these anxious ones, the heavenly angels were continually wafting their wings over them to scatter the thick darkness.

"As the praying ones continued their earnest cries, at times a ray of light from Jesus came to them, to encourage their hearts and light up their countenances. Some, I saw, did not participate in this work of agonizing and pleading. They seemed indifferent and careless. They were not resisting the darkness around them, and it shut them in like a thick cloud. The angels of God left these and went to the aid of the earnest, praying ones. I saw angels of God hasten to the assistance of all who were struggling with all their power to resist the evil angels and trying to help themselves by calling upon God with perseverance. But His angels left those who made no effort to help themselves, and I lost sight of them.

"I asked the meaning of the shaking I had seen and was shown that it would be caused by the straight testimony called forth by the counsel of the True Witness to the Laodiceans. This will have its effect upon the heart of the receiver, and will lead him to exalt the standard and pour forth the straight truth. Some will not bear this straight testimony. They will rise up against it, and this is what will cause a shaking among God's people.

"I saw that the testimony of the True Witness has not been half heeded. The solemn testimony upon which the destiny of the church hangs has been lightly esteemed, if not entirely disregarded. This testimony must work deep repentance; all who truly receive it will obey it and be purified." EW 269-270

17 It Is Our Time Now!

A complete cycle of four generations has passed since 1844. The iniquity of the fathers has been visited, in no uncertain terms, upon the third and fourth generations of Adventism. We are into a fifth generation.

A fifth generation is really a **new** first generation. One complete cycle of sowing and reaping (1844-2004) through four generations has passed and therefore this **first** generation in a **new** cycle presents God's people with another era of opportunity to grasp God's special favour. And, as we saw earlier on, just as God had intended to finish the work early rather than late in that generation, so it is now.

Indeed the time has come again when all Heaven is waiting to be gracious and the angels are excited by the prospect of speedy climax to the Great Controversy very early in this new generation.

It is our time now! Let us not frustrate Jesus anymore. He has been patiently waiting for His wife to make herself ready. He has been patiently waiting for the harvest to ripen. No bride takes forever to get ready and no crop takes forever to ripen. Given the right time and the right conditions even a delayed crop will speedily ripen for the sickle.

As we enter this new generation after 2004 we have all the lessons from the previous four generations and indeed all of past history to draw upon. Let us in repentance, both individual and corporate, accept the light and walk therein. Amazing events are set to occur in the world in the immediate future. Amazing things can also occur among God's remnant people if they accept this time as an "acceptable year of the Lord" and know the hour of their visitation.

The acceptance of the true gospel will enable God's people to walk in the light, experiencing both revival and reformation. They will walk in the light of health reform and, putting away all animal products from their diet, enjoy the blessings of a Genesis 1:29 diet. They will walk in the light of dress reform and enjoy elegance and taste in "well-covered" modesty and simplicity. They will walk in the light of Sabbath reform, finding the Sabbath a delight, guarding its edges and enjoying God's rest because they enjoy His work of victory in their hearts everyday!

A Biblical Case Study On How To Respond In An Acceptable Era

Jeremiah 29:10-14 states clearly how God visits His people with special grace when the time approaches for their **deliverance**.

> *"For thus saith the LORD, That after seventy years shall be accomplished at Babylon I will visit you, and perform my good word towards you, in causing you to return to this place. For I know the thoughts that I think towards you, saith the LORD, thoughts of peace, and not of evil, to give you an expected end. Then shall ye call upon me, and ye shall go and pray to me, and I will hearken to you. And ye shall seek me, and find me, when ye shall search for me with all your heart. And I will be found by you, saith the LORD: and I will turn away your captivity, and I will gather you from all the nations, and from all the places whither I have driven you, saith the LORD: and I will bring you again into the place whence I caused you to be carried away captive."*
> *Jere 29:10-14 (Webster)*

Daniel claimed this promise, he fasted and prayed.

He sent up a prayer of repentance for his entire nation, the professed people of God. He confessed the sins of their fathers in rebelling against God and refusing to listen to God's prophets.

We too must seek the Lord with all our heart in both individual and corporate repentance. We must claim His promises. We must accept the testimony of the prophet and receive the wonderful message of righteousness by faith and walk in the advancing light. Let us read the inspired commentary in *Prophets And Kings* 551-557.

The Return of the Exiles

"The advent of the army of Cyrus before the walls of Babylon was to the Jews a sign that their deliverance from captivity was drawing nigh. More than a century before the birth of Cyrus, Inspiration had mentioned him by name, and had caused a record to be made of the actual work he should do in taking the city of Babylon unawares, and in preparing the way for the release of the children of the captivity. Through Isaiah the word had been spoken:

"Thus saith the Lord to His anointed, to Cyrus, whose right hand I have holden, to subdue nations before him; . . . to open before him the two-leaved gates; and the gates shall not be shut; I will go before thee, and make the crooked places straight: I will break in pieces the gates of brass, and cut in sunder the bars of iron: and I will give thee the treasures of darkness, and hidden riches of secret places, that thou mayest know that I, the Lord, which call thee by thy name, am the God of Israel." Isaiah 45:1-3.

In the unexpected entry of the army of the Persian conqueror into the heart of the Babylonian capital by way of the channel of the river whose waters had been turned aside, and through the inner gates that in careless security had been left open and unprotected, the Jews had abundant evidence of the literal fulfillment of Isaiah's prophecy concerning the sudden overthrow of their oppressors. And this should have been to them an unmistakable sign that God was shaping the affairs of nations in their behalf; for inseparably linked with the prophecy outlining the manner of Babylon's capture and fall were the words:

"Cyrus, he is My shepherd, and shall perform all My pleasure: even saying to Jerusalem, Thou shalt be built; and to the temple, Thy foundation shall be laid." "I have raised him up in righteousness, and I will direct all his ways: he shall build My city, and he shall let go My captives, not for price nor reward, saith the Lord of hosts." Isaiah 44:28; 45:13.

"Nor were these the only prophecies upon which the exiles had opportunity to base their hope of speedy deliverance. The writings of Jeremiah were within their reach, and in these was plainly set forth the length of time that should elapse before the restoration of Israel from Babylon. "When seventy years are accomplished," the Lord had foretold through His messenger, "I will punish the king of Babylon, and that nation, saith the Lord, for their iniquity, and the land of the Chaldeans, and will make it perpetual desolations." Jeremiah 25:12. Favor would be shown the remnant of Judah, in answer to fervent prayer. "I will be found of you, saith the Lord: and I will turn away your captivity, and I will gather you from all the nations, and from all the places whither I have driven you, saith the Lord; and I will bring you again into the place whence I caused you to be carried away captive." Jeremiah 29:14.

"Often had Daniel and his companions gone over these and similar prophecies outlining God's purpose for His people. And now, as the rapid course of events betokened the mighty hand of God at work among the nations, Daniel gave special thought to the promises made to Israel. His faith in the prophetic word led him to enter into experiences foretold by the sacred writers. "After seventy years be accomplished at Babylon," the Lord had declared, "I will visit you, and perform My good word toward you, in causing you to return. . . . I know the thoughts that I think toward you, saith the Lord, thoughts of peace, and not of evil, to give you an expected end. Then shall ye call upon Me, and ye shall go and pray unto Me, and I will hearken unto you. And ye shall seek Me, and find Me, when ye shall search for Me with all your heart." Verses 10-13.

"Shortly before the fall of Babylon, when Daniel was meditating on these prophecies and seeking God for an understanding of the times, a series of visions was given him concerning the rise and fall of kingdoms. With the first vision, as recorded in the seventh chapter of the book of Daniel, an interpretation was given; yet not all was made clear to the prophet. "My cogitations much troubled me," he wrote of his experience at the time, "and my countenance changed in me: but I kept the matter in my heart." Daniel 7:28.

"Through another vision further light was thrown upon the events of the future; and it was at the close of this vision that Daniel heard "one saint speaking, and another saint said unto that certain saint which spake, How long shall be the vision?" Daniel 8:13. The answer that was given, "Unto two thousand and three hundred days; then shall the sanctuary be cleansed" (verse 14), filled him with perplexity. Earnestly he sought for the meaning of the vision. He could not understand the relation sustained by the seventy years' captivity, as foretold through Jeremiah, to the twenty-three hundred years that in vision he heard the heavenly visitant declare should elapse before the cleansing of God's sanctuary. The angel Gabriel gave him a partial interpretation; yet when the prophet heard the words, "The vision . . . shall be for many days," he fainted away. "I Daniel fainted," he records of his experience, "and was sick certain days; afterward I rose up, and did the king's business; and I was astonished at the vision, but none understood it." Verses 26, 27.

"Still burdened in behalf of Israel, Daniel studied anew the prophecies of Jeremiah. They were very plain–so plain that he understood by these testimonies recorded in books "the number of the years, whereof the word of the Lord came to Jeremiah the prophet, that He would accomplish seventy years in the desolations of Jerusalem." Daniel 9:2.

"With faith founded on the sure word of prophecy, Daniel pleaded with the Lord for the speedy fulfillment of these promises. He pleaded for the honor of God to be preserved. In his petition he identified himself fully with those who had fallen short of the divine purpose, confessing their sins as his own.

"I set my face unto the Lord God," the prophet declared, "to seek by prayer and supplications, with fasting, and sackcloth, and ashes: and I prayed unto the Lord my God, and made my confession." Verses 3, 4. Though Daniel had long been in the service of God, and had been spoken of by heaven as "greatly beloved," yet he now appeared before God as a sinner, urging the great need of the people he loved. His prayer was eloquent in its simplicity, and intensely earnest. Hear him pleading:

"O Lord, the great and dreadful God, keeping the covenant and mercy to them that love Him, and to them that keep His commandments; we have sinned, and have committed iniquity, and have done wickedly, and have rebelled, even by departing from Thy precepts and from Thy judgments; neither have we hearkened unto Thy servants the prophets, which spake in Thy name to our kings, our princes, and our fathers, and to all the people of the land.

"O Lord, righteousness belongeth unto Thee, but unto us confusion of faces, as at this day; to the men of Judah, and to the inhabitants of Jerusalem, and unto all Israel, that are near, and that are far off, through all the countries whither Thou hast driven them, because of their trespass that they have trespassed against Thee.

"To the Lord our God belong mercies and forgiveness, though we have rebelled against Him." "O Lord, according to all Thy righteousness, I beseech Thee, let Thine anger and Thy fury be turned away from Thy city Jerusalem, Thy holy mountain: because for our sins, and for the iniquities of our fathers, Jerusalem and Thy people are become a reproach to all that are about us.

"Now therefore, O our God, hear the prayer of Thy servant, and his supplications, and cause Thy face to shine upon Thy sanctuary that is desolate, for the Lord's sake. O my God, incline Thine ear, and hear; open Thine eyes, and behold our desolations, and the city which is called by Thy name: for we do not present our supplications before Thee for our righteousness, but for Thy great mercies.

*"O Lord, hear; O Lord, forgive; O Lord, hearken and do; defer
not, for Thine own sake, O my God: for Thy city and Thy people
are called by Thy name." Verses 4-9, 16-19.*

"Heaven was bending low to hear the earnest supplication of
the prophet. Even before he had finished his plea for pardon
and restoration, the mighty Gabriel again appeared to him,
and called his attention to the vision he had seen prior to
the fall of Babylon and the death of Belshazzar. And then the
angel outlined before him in detail the period of the seventy
weeks, which was to begin at the time of "the going forth of the
commandment to restore and to build Jerusalem." Verse 25.

"Daniel's prayer had been offered "in the first year of Darius"
(verse 1), the Median monarch whose general, Cyrus, had
wrested from Babylonia the scepter of universal rule. The
reign of Darius was honored of God. To him was sent the
angel Gabriel, "to confirm and to strengthen him." Daniel 11:1.
Upon his death, within about two years of the fall of Babylon,
Cyrus succeeded to the throne, and the beginning of his reign
marked the completion of the seventy years since the first
company of Hebrews had been taken by Nebuchadnezzar from
their Judean home to Babylon.

"The deliverance of Daniel from the den of lions had been
used of God to create a favorable impression upon the mind
of Cyrus the Great. The sterling qualities of the man of God as
a statesman of farseeing ability led the Persian ruler to show
him marked respect and to honor his judgment. And now,
just at the time God had said He would cause His temple at
Jerusalem to be rebuilt, He moved upon Cyrus as His agent to
discern the prophecies concerning himself, with which Daniel
was so familiar, and to grant the Jewish people their liberty.

"As the king saw the words foretelling, more than a hundred
years before his birth, the manner in which Babylon should
be taken; as he read the message addressed to him by the
Ruler of the universe, "I girded thee, though thou hast not
known Me: that they may know from the rising of the sun,
and from the west, that there is none beside Me;" as he saw
before his eyes the declaration of the eternal God, "For Jacob

My servant's sake, and Israel Mine elect, I have even called thee by thy name: I have surnamed thee, though thou hast not known Me;" as he traced the inspired record, "I have raised him up in righteousness, and I will direct all his ways: he shall build My city, and he shall let go My captives, not for price nor reward," his heart was profoundly moved, and he determined to fulfill his divinely appointed mission. Isaiah 45:5, 6, 4, 13. He would let the Judean captives go free; he would help them restore the temple of Jehovah.

"In a written proclamation published "throughout all his kingdom," Cyrus made known his desire to provide for the return of the Hebrews and for the rebuilding of their temple. "The Lord God of heaven hath given me all the kingdoms of the earth," the king gratefully acknowledged in this public proclamation; "and He hath charged me to build Him an house at Jerusalem, which is in Judah. Who is there among you of all His people? his God be with him, and let him go up to Jerusalem, . . . and build the house of the Lord God of Israel, (He is the God,) which is in Jerusalem. And whosoever remaineth in any place where he sojourneth, let the men of his place help him with silver, and with gold, and with goods, and with beasts, beside the freewill offering." Ezra 1:1-4.

"Let the house be builded," he further directed regarding the temple structure, "the place where they offered sacrifices, and let the foundations thereof be strongly laid; the height thereof threescore cubits, and the breadth thereof threescore cubits; with three rows of great stones, and a row of new timber: and let the expenses be given out of the king's house: and also let the golden and silver vessels of the house of God, which Nebuchadnezzar took forth out of the temple which is at Jerusalem, and brought unto Babylon, be restored, and brought again unto the temple which is at Jerusalem." Ezra 6:3-5." PK 551-557

"Let all remember that the mysteries of God's kingdom cannot be learned by reasoning. True faith, true prayer–how strong they are! The prayer of the Pharisee had no value, but the prayer of the publican was heard in the courts above, because it showed dependence reaching forth to lay hold of Omnipotence. **Self was to the publican nothing but shame. Thus it must be with all who seek God. Faith and prayer are the two arms which the needy suppliant lays upon the neck of infinite Love.**

"We are saved by hope: but hope that is seen is not hope: for what a man seeth, why doth he yet hope for? But if we hope for that we see not, then do we with patience wait for it. Likewise the Spirit also helpeth our infirmities: for we know not what we should pray for as we ought: but the Spirit itself maketh intercession for us with groanings which can not be uttered. And he that searcheth the hearts knoweth what is the mind of the Spirit, because he maketh intercession for the saints according to the will of God. And we know that all things work together for good to them that love God, to them who are the called according to his purpose. . . . What shall we then say to these things? If God be for us, who can be against us? He that spared not his own Son, but delivered him up for us all, how shall he not with him also freely give us all things? . . . I am persuaded, that neither death, nor life, nor angels, nor principalities, nor powers, not things present, not things to come, nor height, nor depth, nor any other creature, shall be able to separate us from the love of God, which is in Christ Jesus our Lord."

"Let us commit the needs of the soul to him who has loved us, and given his precious life that he might make it possible for us to learn of him. While lifting the cross, he says to us, "If any man will come after me, let him deny himself, and take up his cross daily, and follow me." Christ alone can make us capable of responding when he says, "Take my yoke upon you, and learn of me; for I am meek and lowly in heart." **This means that every day self must be denied. Christ can give us the noble resolve, the will to suffer, and to fight the battles of the Lord with persevering energy. The weakest, aided by divine grace, may have strength to be more than conqueror."**
RH Oct 30, 1900

18 Changed Into His Image

E.G. White: Review and Herald, 4-28-1891

"Sin-burdened, struggling souls, Jesus in his glorified humanity has ascended into the heavens to make intercession for us. "For we have not a high priest which cannot be touched with the feeling of our infirmities; but was in all points tempted like as we are, yet without sin. Let us therefore come boldly unto the throne of grace." We should be continually looking unto Jesus, the author and finisher of our faith; for by beholding him we shall be changed into his image, our character will be made like his. We should rejoice that all judgment is given to the Son, because in his humanity he has become acquainted with all the difficulties that beset humanity.

"To be sanctified is to become a partaker of the divine nature, catching the spirit and mind of Jesus, ever learning in the school of Christ. "But we all with open face beholding as in a glass the glory of the Lord, are changed into the same image from glory to glory, even as of the Lord the Spirit." It is impossible for any of us by our power or our own efforts to work this change in ourselves. It is the Holy Spirit, the Comforter, which Jesus said He would send into the world, that changes our character into the image of Christ; and when this is accomplished, we reflect, as in a mirror, the glory of the Lord. That is, the character of the one who thus beholds Christ is so like his, that one looking at his sees Christ's own character shining out as from a mirror. Imperceptibly to ourselves, we are changed day by day from our own ways and will into the ways and will of Christ, into the loveliness of his character. Thus we grow up into Christ, and unconsciously reflect his image.

"Professed Christians keep altogether too near the lowlands of earth. Their eyes are trained to see only common-place things, and their minds dwell upon the things their eyes behold. Their religious experience is often shallow and unsatisfying, and their words are light and valueless. How can such reflect the image of Christ? How can they send forth the bright beams of the Sun of Righteousness into all the dark places of the earth? To be a Christian is to be Christ-like.

"Enoch kept the Lord ever before him, and the inspired word says that he "walked with God." He made Christ his constant companion. He was in the world, and performed his duties to the world; but he was ever under the influence of Jesus. He reflected Christ's character, exhibiting the same qualities in goodness, mercy, tender compassion, sympathy, forbearance, meekness, humility, and love. His association with Christ day by day transformed him into the image of him with whom he was so intimately connected. Day by day he was growing away from his own way into Christ's way, the heavenly, the divine, in his thoughts and feelings. He was constantly inquiring. "Is this the way of the Lord?" His was a constant growth, and he had fellowship with the Father and the Son. This is genuine sanctification.

"Many who claim to be sanctified become boisterous, passionate, and wholly unlike Christ in words and deportment, if their will is crossed. These show that they are not what they claim to be.

The more closely one views Christ, the less disposed will be to make high claims to holiness He will have a humble opinion of himself and of his own goodness, but Christ will be revealed in his character.

"Christ said, "It is expedient for you that I go away." No one could then have any preference because of his location or personal contact with Christ. The Saviour would be accessible to all alike, spiritually, and in this sense he would be nearer to us all than if he had not ascended on high. Now all may be equally favored by beholding him and reflecting his character. The eye of faith sees him ever present, in all his goodness, grace forbearance, courtesy, and love, those spiritual and divine attributes. *And as we behold, we are changed into his likeness.*

"Christ is soon coming in the clouds of heaven, and we must be prepared to meet him, not having spot or wrinkle or any such thing. We are now to accept the invitation of Christ. He says, "Come unto me, all ye that labor and are heavy laden, and I will give you rest. Take my yoke upon you, and learn of me; for I am meek and lowly in heart; and ye shall find rest unto your souls." The words of Christ to Nicodemus are of practical value to us to-day: "Except a man be born of water and of the Spirit, he cannot enter into the kingdom of God. That which is born of the flesh is flesh; and that which is born of the Spirit is spirit. Marvel not that I said unto thee, Ye must be born again. The wind bloweth where it listeth, and thou hearest the sound thereof, but canst not tell whence it cometh, and whither it goeth: so is every one that is born of the Spirit."

"The converting power of God must be upon our hearts. We must study the life of Christ, and imitate the divine Pattern. We must dwell upon the perfection of his character, and be changed into his image. No one will enter the kingdom of God unless his passions are subdued, unless his will is brought into captivity to the will of Christ.

"Heaven is free from all sin, from all defilement and impurity; and if we would live in its atmosphere, if we would behold the glory of Christ, we must be pure in heart, perfect in character through his grace and righteousness. We must not be taken up with pleasure and amusement, but be fitting up for the glorious mansions Christ has gone to prepare for us. If we are faithful, seeking to bless others, patient in well-doing, at his coming Christ will crown us with glory, honor,and immortality.

"Prophecy reveals the fact that we are nearing the end of all things, and the people of God are to be the light of the world. In character and life we are to make manifest the requirement of God in humanity; and in order to do this, we must gather up the rays of divine light from the Bible, and let them shine forth to those who are in darkness. Christ must abide in our hearts by faith, that we may know and teach the way to heaven. "And they that be wise shall shine as the brightness of the firmament; and they that turn many to righteousness, as the stars forever and ever."

"Christ is soon coming in glory, and when his majesty is revealed, the world will wish that they had his favor. At that time we shall all desire a place in the mansions of heaven; but those who do not confess Christ now in word, in life, in character, cannot expect that he will confess them then before his Father and the holy angels. By those who have denied him, the cry will be raised, even to the mountains, "Fall on us, and hide us from the face of him that sitteth on the throne, and from the wrath of the Lamb: for the great day of his wrath is come; and who shall be able to stand?" O, how happy will those be who have made themselves ready for the marriage supper of the Lamb, who are robed in the righteousness of Christ, and reflect his lovely image! They will have on the pure white linen which is the righteousness of the saints, and Christ will lead them by the side of living waters; God will wipe away all tears from their eyes, and they will have the life that runs parallel with the life of God." RH 4-28-1891

Appendix A

Additional References

Sermon No. 13, 1895: A.T. Jones

The particular thought which will be the subject of our study at this time is that which is found in the 11th verse, second chapter of Hebrews: "Both he that sanctifieth and they who are sanctified are all of one." It is men of this world, sinful men, whom Christ sanctifies —He is the Sanctifier. And He and these are all of one.

In this part of the chapter you will remember we are studying man. In the first chapter, as we have seen, there is shown the contrast between Christ and the angels with Christ above the angels as God. In the second chapter the contrast is between Christ and the angels with Christ below the angels. God has not put in subjection to the angels the world to come whereof we speak. He has put it in subjection to man and Christ is the man. Therefore Christ became man; He takes the place of man; He was born as man is born. In His human nature Christ came from the man from whom we all have come, so that the expression in this verse, "all of one," is the same as "all from one —as all coming forth from one. One man is the source and head of all our human nature. And the genealogy of Christ, as one of us, runs to Adam. Luke 3:38.

It is true that all men and all things are from God, but the thought in this chapter is man, and Christ as man. We are the sons of the first man, and so is Christ according to the flesh. We are now studying Christ in His human nature. The first chapter of Hebrews is Christ in His divine nature. The second chapter is Christ in human nature. The thought in these two chapters is clearly akin to that in the second chapter of Philippians, verses 5-8:

Let this mind be in you which was also in Christ Jesus: who, being in the form of God, thought it not robbery to be equal with God: but made himself of no reputation, and took upon him the form of a servant, and was made in the likeness of men: and being found in fashion as a man, he humbled himself, and became obedient unto death, even the death of the cross.

In that passage Christ in the two forms is set forth. First, being in the form of God, He took the form of man. In Hebrews, first two chapters, it is not the form but the nature.

I repeat: In the second chapter of Philippians we have Christ in the two forms —the form of God and the form of man. In Hebrews, first and second chapters, we have Christ in the two natures, the nature of God and the nature of man. You may have something in the form of man that would not be of the nature of man. You can have a piece of stone in the form of man, but it is not the nature of man. Jesus Christ took the form of man, that is true, and He did more; He took the nature of man.

Let us read now the fourteenth verse of the second chapter of Hebrews. Forasmuch then as the children [the children of Adam, the human race] are partakers of flesh and blood, He also Himself likewise took part of the same. "Likewise means in this wise, in this way, in a way like this which is spoken of. Therefore Christ took flesh and blood in a way like we take it. But how did we take flesh and blood? —By birth and clear from Adam too. He took flesh and blood by birth also and clear from Adam too. For it is written: He is the seed of David according to the flesh. Romans 1: 3. While David calls Him Lord, He also is David's son. Matt. 22:42-45. His genealogy is traced to David, but it does not stop there. It goes to Abraham, because He is the seed of Abraham. He took on Him the seed of Abraham, as in the sixteenth verse of this second chapter of Hebrews. Nor does His genealogy stop with Abraham; it goes to Adam. Luke 3:38. Therefore He which sanctifieth among men and they who are sanctified among men are all of one. All coming from one man according to the flesh, are all of one. Thus on the human side, Christ's nature is precisely our nature.

Let us look at the other side again for an illustration of this oneness, that we may see the force of this expression that He and we are all of one.

On the other side, however, as in the first chapter of Hebrews, He is of the nature of God. The name God which He bears belongs to Him by the very fact of His existence; it belongs to Him by inheritance.As that name belongs to Him entirely because He exists and as certainly as He exists and as it belongs to Him by nature, it is certain that His nature is the nature of God.

Also, in the first chapter of John, first verse, it is written: "In the beginning was the Word, and the Word was with God. That word "with" does not express the reality of the thought as well as another. The German puts a word in there that defines the Greek closer than ours does. That says, "In the beginning was the Word, and the Word was bei God" literally, "The Word was of God." And that is true. The Greek word conveys the same idea as that my right arm is of me, of my body. The Greek therefore is literally, In the beginning "the word was God."

This simply illustrates on that side the fact as to what He is on this side. For as on the divine side, He was of God, of the nature of God, and was really God, so on the human side He is of man and of the nature of man and really man.

Look at the fourteenth verse of the first chapter of John. "And the Word was made flesh and dwelt among us." That tells the same story that we are reading here in the first two chapters of Hebrews. "In the beginning was the Word, and the Word was of God, and the Word was God." "And the Word was made flesh, and dwelt among us" —flesh and blood as ours is.

Now what kind of flesh is it? What kind of flesh alone is it that this world knows? Just such flesh as you and I have. This world does not know any other flesh of man and has not known any other since the necessity for Christs coming was created. Therefore, as this world knows only such flesh as we have, as it is now, it is certainly true that when the Word was made flesh," He was made just as flesh as ours is. It cannot be otherwise.

Again: What kind of flesh is our flesh, as it is in itself? Let us turn to the eighth chapter of Romans and read whether Christ's human nature meets ours and is as ours in that respect wherein ours is sinful flesh. Romans 8:3: "What the law could not do in that it was weak through the flesh, God sending his own Son" did.

There was something that the law could not do, and that God, sending His own Son, did. But why was it that the law could not do what it desired and what was required? It was weak through the flesh. The trouble was in the flesh. It was this that caused the law to fail of its purpose concerning man. Then God sent Christ to do what the law could not do. And the law having failed of its purpose because of the flesh and not because of any lack in itself, God must send Him to help the flesh and not to help the law. If the law had been in itself too weak to do what it was intended to do, then the thing for Him to have done to help the matter out would be to remedy the law. But the trouble was with the flesh, and therefore He must remedy the flesh.

It is true that the argument nowadays, springing up from that enmity that is against God and is not subject to the law of God, neither indeed can be, is that the law could not do what was intended and God sent His Son to weaken the law, so that the flesh could answer the demands of the law. But if I am weak and you are strong and I need help, it does not help me any to make you as weak as I am; I am as weak and helpless as before. There is no help at all in all that. But when I am weak and you are strong and you can bring to me your strength, that helps me. So the law was strong enough, but its purpose could not be accomplished through the weakness of the flesh. Therefore God, to supply the need, must bring strength to weak flesh. He sent Christ to supply the need and therefore Christ must so arrange it that strength may be brought to our flesh itself which we have today, that the purpose of the law may be met in our flesh. So it is written: "God sending his own Son in the likeness of sinful flesh," in order "that the righteousness of the law might be fulfilled in us, who walk not after the flesh, but after the Spirit."

Now do not get a wrong idea of that word likeness. It is not the shape; it is not the photograph; it is not the likeness in the sense of an image, but it is likeness in the sense of being like indeed. The word likeness here is not the thought that is in the second chapter of Philippians, where it is shape, the form, or likeness as to form, but here in the book of Hebrews it is likeness in nature, likeness to the flesh as it is in itself, God sending His own Son in that which is just like sinful flesh. And in order to be just like sinful flesh, it would have to be sinful flesh; in order to be made flesh at all, as it is in this world, He would have to be just such flesh as it is in this world, just such as we have and that is sinful flesh. This is what is said in the words "likeness of sinful flesh."

This is shown in the ninth and tenth verses of Hebrews 2, also: "We see Jesus, who was made a little lower than the angels"—not only as man was made lower than the angels when He was created.

Man was sinless when God made him a little lower than the angels. That was sinless flesh. But man fell from that place and condition and became sinful flesh.

Now we see Jesus, who was made a little lower than the angels, but not as man was made when he was first made a little lower than the angels, but as man is since he sinned and became still lower than the angels. That is where we see Jesus. Let us read and see: We see Jesus who was made a little lower than the angels. What for? "For the suffering of death." Then Christ's being made as much lower than the angels as man is, is as much lower than the angels as man is since he sinned and became subject to death. We see him "crowned with glory and honor; that he by the grace of God should taste death for every man. For it became him [it was appropriate for him], for whom are all things and by whom are all things in bringing many sons unto glory, to make the captain of their salvation perfect through sufferings."

Therefore, as He became subject to suffering and death, this demonstrates strongly enough that the point lower than the angels at which Christ came to stand; where He does stand and where "we see him," is the point to which man came when he, in sin, stepped still lower than where God made him —even then a little lower than the angels.

Again: the sixteenth verse: "Verily he took not on him the nature of angels, but he took on him the seed of Abraham. He took not on him the nature of angels but he took on Him the nature of Abraham. But the nature of Abraham and of the seed of Abraham is only human nature.

Again: "Wherefore in all things it behooved him to be made like unto his brethren." In how many things? All things. Then in His human nature there is not a particle of difference between Him and you.

Let us read the scripture. Let us study this closely. I want to see that we shall stand by it. Let us read it over: "Are all of one." He took part of flesh and blood in the same way that we take part of flesh and blood. He took not the nature of angels but the seed, the nature, of Abraham. Wherefore —for these reasons —it behooved Him —what is behooved? It was the proper thing for Him to do —it became Him, it was appropriate. It behooved Him to be made in all things like unto His brethren. Who are His brethren, though? —The human race. "All of one," and for this cause He is not ashamed to call them brethren. Because we are all of one, He is not ashamed to call you and me brethren. Wherefore in all things it behooved Him to be made like unto His brethren."

Well, then, in His human nature, when He was upon the earth, was He in any wise different from what you are in your human nature tonight? [A few in the congregation responded, "NO"] I wish we had heard everybody in the house say, "no," with a loud voice. You are too timid altogether. The word of God says that, and we are to say, That is so, because there is salvation in just that one thing. No, it is not enough to say it that way: the salvation of God for human beings lies in just that one thing. We are not to be timid about it at all. There our salvation lies, and until we get there we are not sure of our salvation. That is where it is. "In all things it behooved him to be made like unto his brethren." What for? —O, "that he might be a merciful and faithful high priest in things pertaining to God, to make reconciliation for the sins of the people. For in that He Himself hath suffered being tempted, He is able to succor them that are tempted." Then don't you see that our salvation lies just there? Do you not see that it is right there where Christ comes to us? He came to us just where we are tempted and was made like us just where we are tempted, and there is the point where we meet Him—the living Saviour against the power of temptation.

Now the fourteenth verse of the fourth chapter of Hebrews:

Seeing then that we have a great high priest that is passed into the heavens, Jesus, the Son of God, let us hold fast our profession. For we have not a high priest which cannot be touched with the feeling of our infirmities; but was in all points tempted like as we are.

He could not have been tempted in all points like as I am if He were not in all points like as I am to start with. Therefore it behooved Him to be made in all points like me, if He is going to help me where I need help. I know that right there is where I need it. And oh, I know it is right there where I get it. Thank the Lord! There is where Christ stands and there is my help.

"We have not a high priest which cannot be touched"—two negatives there; have not a high priest which cannot be touched. Then what do we have on the affirmative side? We have a high priest who can be touched with the feeling of our infirmities—my infirmities, your infirmities, our infirmities. Does He feel my infirmities? Yes. Does He feel your infirmities? Yes. What is an infirmity? Weakness, wavering, weakness —that is expressive enough. We have many of them. All of us have many of them. We feel our weaknesses. Thank the Lord, there is One who feels them also —yea, not only feels them but is touched with the feeling of them. There is more in that word "touched" than simply that He is reached with the feeling of our weaknesses and feels as we feel. He feels as we feel, that is true, but beyond that He is "touched"; that is, He is tenderly affected; His sympathy is stirred. He is touched to tenderness and affected to sympathy and He helps us. This is what is said in the words, "touched with the feeling of our infirmities." Thank the Lord for such a Saviour!

But I say again, He cannot be tempted in all points like as I am unless He was in all points like I am to start with. He could not feel as I do unless He is where I am and as I am. In other words, He could not be tempted in all points as I am and feel as I feel unless He was just myself over again. The word of God says: "In all points like as we are."

Let us study this further. There are things that will tempt you strongly that will draw hard on you, that are no more to me than a zephyr in a summer day. Something will draw hard on me, even to my overthrowing, that would not affect you at all. What strongly tempts one may not affect another. Then, in order to help me, Jesus must be where He can feel what I feel and be tempted in all points where I could be tempted with any power at all. What strongly tempts one may not affect another. Then, in order to help me, Jesus must be where He can feel what I feel and be tempted in all points where I could be tempted with any power at all. But as things that tempt me may not affect you at all and things that affect you may not affect me, Christ has to stand where you and I both are, so as to meet all the temptations of both. He must feel all those which you meet that do not affect me and also all those which I meet that do not affect you. He has to take the place of both of us. That is so.

Then there is the other man. There are things that tempt him to his overthrow that do not affect you or me either. Then Jesus had to take all the feelings and nature of myself, of yourself, and of the other man also, so that He could be tempted in all points like as I am and in all points like as you are and in all points like as the other man is. But when you and I and the other man are taken in Him, how many does that embrace? That takes the whole human race.

And this is exactly the truth. Christ was in the place and He had the nature of the whole human race. And in Him meet all the weaknesses of mankind, so that every man on earth who can be tempted at all finds in Jesus Christ power against temptation. For every soul there is in Jesus Christ victory against all temptation and relief from the power of it. That is the truth.

Let us look at it from another side. There is one in the world —Satan, the god of this world —who is interested in seeing that we are tempted just as much as possible, but he does not have to employ much of his time nor very much of his power in temptation to get us to yield.

That same one was here and he was particularly interested in getting Jesus to yield to temptation. He tried Jesus upon every point upon which he would ever have to try me to get me to sin, and he tried in vain. He utterly failed to get Jesus to consent to sin in any single point upon which I can ever be tempted.

He also tried Jesus upon every point upon which he has ever tried you or ever can try you to get you to sin, and he utterly failed there too. That takes you and me both then, and Jesus has conquered in all points for both you and me.

But when he tried Jesus upon all the points that he has tried upon both you and me and failed there, as he did completely fail, he had to try Him more than that yet. He had to try Him upon all the points upon which he has tried the other man to get him to yield. Satan did this also and also there completely failed.

Thus Satan had to try, and he did try, Jesus upon all the points that he ever had to try me upon and upon all the points that he ever had to try you upon and also upon all the points that he would have to try the other man upon. Consequently he had to try Jesus upon every point upon which it is possible for a temptation to rise in any man of the human race.

Satan is the author of all temptation, and he had to try Jesus upon every point upon which it is possible for Satan himself to raise a temptation. And in all he failed all the time. Thank the Lord!

More than that: Satan not only had to try Jesus upon all the points where he has ever had to try me, but he had to try Jesus with a good deal more power than he ever had to exert upon me. He never had to try very hard nor use very much of his power in temptation to get me to yield. But taking the same points upon which Satan has ever tried me in which he got me to sin or would ever have to try to get me to sin, he had to try Jesus on those same points a good deal harder than he ever did to get me to sin. He had to try him with all the power of temptation that he possibly knows —that is, the devil I mean —and failed. Thank the Lord! So in Christ I am free.

He had to try Jesus in all points where he ever tempted or ever can tempt you and he had to try Him with all the power that he knows, and he failed again. Thank the Lord! So you are free in Christ. He had also to try Jesus upon every point that affects the other man with all his Satanic power also, and still he failed. Thank the Lord! And in Christ the other man is free.

Therefore he had to try Jesus upon every point that ever the human could be tried upon and failed. He had to try Jesus with all the knowledge that he has and all the cunning that he knows and failed. And he had to try Jesus with all his might upon each particular point, and still he failed.

Then there is a threefold —yes, a complete —failure on the devil's part all around., In the presence of Christ, Satan is absolutely conquered, and in Christ we are conquerors of Satan. Jesus said, "The prince of this world cometh, and hath nothing in me." In Christ, then, we escape him. In Christ we meet in Satan a completely conquered and a completely exhausted enemy.

This is not to say that we have no more fighting to do. But it is to say and to say emphatically and joyfully that in Christ we fight the fight of victory. Out of Christ, we fight —but it is all defeat. In Him our victory is complete, as well as in all things in Him we are complete. But, O do not forget the expression: It is in Him!

Then, as Satan has exhausted all the temptations that he knows or possibly can know and has exhausted all his power in the temptation too, what is he? In the presence of Christ, what is he? Powerless. And when he finds us in Christ and then would reach us and harass us, what is he? Powerless. Praise and magnify the Lord!

Let us rejoice in this, for in Him we are victors; in Him we are free; in Him Satan is powerless toward us. Let us be thankful for that. In Him we are complete." A.T. Jones 1895

How to Meet a Controverted Point of Doctrine: A.T. Jones

"We want to understand the time in which we live. We do not half understand it. We do not half take it in. My heart trembles in me when I think of what a foe we have to meet, and how poorly we are prepared to meet him. The trials of the children of Israel, and their attitude just before the first coming of Christ, have been presented before me again and again to illustrate the position of the people of God in their experience before the second coming of Christ. How the enemy sought every occasion to take control of the minds of the Jews, and to-day he is seeking to blind the minds of God's servants, that they may not be able to discern the precious truth.

When Christ came to our world, Satan was on the ground, and disputed every inch of advance in his path from the manger to Calvary. Satan had accused God of requiring self-denial of the angels, when he knew nothing of what it meant himself, and when he would not himself make any self-sacrifice for others. This was the accusation that Satan made against God in heaven; and after the evil one was expelled from heaven, he continually charged the Lord with exacting service which he would not render himself. Christ came to the world to meet these false accusations, and to reveal the Father. We cannot conceive of the humiliation he endured in taking our nature upon himself. Not that in itself it was a disgrace to belong to the human race, but he was the Majesty of heaven, the King of glory, and he humbled himself to become a babe and suffer the wants and woes of mortals. He humbled himself not to the highest position, to be a man of riches and power, but though he was rich, yet for our sake he became poor, that we through his poverty might be made rich. He took step after step in humiliation. He was driven from city to city; for men would not receive the Light of the world. They were perfectly satisfied with their position.

Christ had given precious gems of truth, but men had bound them up in the rubbish of superstition and error. He had imparted to them the words of life, but they did not live by every word that proceeds out of the mouth of God. He saw that the world could not find the word of God, for it was hidden by the traditions of men. He came to place before the world the relative importance of heaven and earth, and put truth in its own place. Jesus alone could reveal the truth which it was necessary men should know in order that they might obtain salvation. He only could place it in the frame-work of truth, and it was his work to free it from error and to set it before men in its heavenly light.

Satan was roused to oppose him, for had he not put forth every effort since the fall to make light appear darkness, and darkness light? As Christ sought to place truth before the people in its proper relation to their salvation, Satan worked through the Jewish leaders, and inspired them with enmity against the Redeemer of the world. They determined to do all in their power to prevent him from making an impression upon the people.

O, how Christ longed, how his heart burned, to open to the priests the greater treasures of the truth! But their minds had been cast in such a mold that it was next to an impossibility to reveal to them the truths relating to his kingdom. The Scriptures had not been read aright. The Jews had been looking for the advent of the Messiah, but they had thought he must come in all the glory that will attend his second appearing. Because he did not come with all the majesty of a king, they utterly refused him. But it was not simply because he did not come in splendor that they refused him. It was because he was the embodiment of purity, and they were impure. He walked the earth a man of spotless integrity. Such a character in the midst of degradation and evil, was out of harmony with their desires, and he was abused and despised. His spotless life flashed light upon the hearts of men, and discovered iniquity to them in its odious character.

The Son of God was assaulted at every step by the powers of darkness. After his baptism he was driven of the Spirit into the wilderness, and suffered temptation for forty days. Letters have been coming in to me, affirming that Christ could not have had the same nature as man, for if he had, he would have fallen under similar temptations. If he did not have man's nature, he could not be our example. If he was not a partaker of our nature, he could not have been tempted as man has been. If it were not possible for him to yield to temptation, he could not be our helper. It was a solemn reality that Christ came to fight the battles as man, in man's behalf. His temptation and victory tell us that humanity must copy the Pattern; man must become a partaker of the divine nature.

In Christ, divinity and humanity were combined. Divinity was not degraded to humanity; divinity held its place, but humanity by being united to divinity, withstood the fiercest test of temptation in the wilderness. The prince of this world came to Christ after his long fast, when he was an hungered, and suggested to him to command the stones to become bread. But the plan of God, devised for the salvation of man, provided that Christ should know hunger, and poverty, and every phase of man's experience. He withstood the temptation, through the power that man may command. He laid hold on the throne of God, and there is not a man or woman who may not have access to the same help through faith in God. Man may become a partaker of the divine nature; not a soul lives who may not summon the aid of Heaven in temptation and trial. Christ came to reveal the Source of his power, that man might never rely on his unaided human capabilities.

Those who would overcome must put to the tax every power of their being. They must agonize on their knees before God for divine power. Christ came to be our example, and to make known to us that we may be partakers of the divine nature. How?–By having escaped the corruptions that are in the world through lust. Satan did not gain the victory over Christ. He did not put his foot upon the soul of the Redeemer. He did not touch the head though he bruised the heel. Christ, by his own example, made it evident that man may stand in integrity. Men may have a power to resist evil–a power that neither earth, nor death, nor hell can master; a power that will place them where they may overcome as Christ overcame. Divinity and humanity may be combined in them.

It was the work of Christ to present the truth in the frame-work of the gospel, and to reveal the precepts and principles that he had given to fallen man. Every idea he presented was his own. He needed not to borrow thoughts from any, for he was the originator of all truth. He could present the ideas of prophets and philosophers, and preserve his originality; for all wisdom was his;

he was the source, the fountain, of all truth. He was in advance of all, and by his teaching he became the spiritual leader for all ages.

It was Christ that spoke through Melchisedec, the priest of the most high God. Melchisedec was not Christ, but he was the voice of God in the world, the representative of the Father. And all through the generations of the past, Christ has spoken; Christ has led his people, and has been the light of the world. When God chose Abraham as a representative of his truth, he took him out of his country, and away from his kindred, and set him apart. He desired to mold him after his own model. He desired to teach him according to his own plan. The mold of the world's teachers was not to be upon him. He was to be taught how to command his children and his household after him, to keep the way of the Lord, to do justice and judgment. This is the work that God would have us do. He would have us understand how to govern our families, how to control our children, how to command our households to keep the way of the Lord.

John was called to do a special work; he was to prepare the way of the Lord, to make straight his paths. The Lord did not send him to the school of the prophets and rabbis. He took him away from the assemblies of men to the desert, that he might learn of nature and nature's God. God did not desire him to have the mold of the priests and rulers. He was called to do a special work. The Lord gave him his message. Did he go to the priests and rulers and ask if he might proclaim this message?–No, God put him away from them that he might not be influenced by their spirit and teaching. He was the voice of one crying in the wilderness, "Prepare ye the way of the Lord, make straight in the desert a highway for our God. Every valley shall be exalted, and every mountain and hill shall be made low: and the crooked shall be made straight, and the rough places plain: and the glory of the Lord shall be revealed, and all flesh shall see it together: for the mouth of the Lord hath spoken it." This is the very message that must be given to our people; we are near the end of time, and the message is, Clear the King's highway; gather out the stones; raise up a standard for the people. The people must be awakened. It is no time now to cry peace and safety. We are exhorted to "cry aloud, spare not, lift up thy voice like a trumpet, and shew my people their transgression, and the house of Jacob their sins."

The light of the glory of God shone upon our Representative, and this fact says to us that the glory of God may shine upon us. With his human arm, Jesus encircled the race, and with his divine arm he grasped the throne of the Infinite, connecting man with God, and earth with heaven.

The light of the glory of God must fall upon us. We need the holy unction from on high. However intelligent, however learned a man may be, he is not qualified to teach unless he has a firm hold on the God of Israel. He who is connected with Heaven will do the works of Christ. By faith in God he will have power to move upon humanity. He will seek for the lost sheep of the house of Israel. If divine power does not combine with human effort, I would not give a straw for all that the greatest man could do. The Holy Spirit is wanting in our work. Nothing frightens me more than to see the spirit of variance manifested by our brethren. We are on dangerous ground when we cannot meet together like Christians, and courteously examine controverted points. I feel like fleeing from the place lest I receive the mold of those who cannot candidly investigate the doctrines of the Bible. Those who cannot impartially examine the evidences of a position that differs from theirs, are not fit to teach in any department of God's cause. What we need is the baptism of the Holy Spirit. Without this, we are no more fitted to go forth to the world than were the disciples after the crucifixion of their Lord. Jesus knew their destitution, and told them to tarry in Jerusalem until they should be endowed with power from on high. Every teacher must be a learner, that his eyes may be anointed to see the evidences of the advancing truth of God. The beams of the Sun of Righteousness must shine into his own heart if he would impart light to others.

No one is able to explain the Scriptures without the aid of the Holy Spirit. But when you take up the word of God with a humble, teachable heart, the angels of God will be by your side to impress you with evidences of the truth. When the Spirit of God rests upon you, there will be no feeling of envy or jealousy in examining another's position; there will be no spirit of accusation and criticism, such as Satan inspired in the hearts of the Jewish leaders against Christ. As Christ said to Nicodemus, so I say to you, "Ye must be born again." "Except a man be born again, he cannot see the kingdom of God." You must have the divine mold before you can discern the sacred claims of the truth. Unless the teacher is a learner in the school of Christ, he is not fitted to teach others.

We should come into a position where every difference will be melted away. If I think I have light, I shall do my duty in presenting it. Suppose I consulted others concerning the message the Lord would have me give to the people, the door might be closed so that the light might not reach the ones to whom God had sent it. When Jesus rode into Jerusalem, "the whole multitude of disciples began to rejoice and praise God with a loud voice for all the mighty works that they had seen; saying, Blessed be the King that cometh in the name of the Lord. Peace in heaven, and glory in the highest. And some of the Pharisees from among the multitude said unto him, Master, rebuke thy disciples. And he answered and said unto them, I tell you that, if these should hold their peace, the stones would immediately cry out.

The Jews tried to stop the proclamation of the message that had been predicted in the word of God; but prophecy must be fulfilled. The Lord says, "Behold, I send you Elijah the prophet, before the coming of the great and dreadful day of the Lord." Somebody is to come in the spirit and power of Elijah, and when he appears, men may say, "You are too earnest, you do not interpret the Scriptures in the proper way. Let me tell you how to teach your message."

There are many who cannot distinguish between the work of God and that of man. I shall tell the truth as God gives it to me, and I say now, If you continue to find fault, to have a spirit of variance, you will never know the truth. Jesus said to his disciples, "I have yet many things to say unto you, but ye cannot bear them now." They were not in a condition to appreciate sacred and eternal things; but Jesus promised to send the Comforter, who would teach them all things, and bring all things to their remembrance, whatsoever he had said unto them. Brethren, we must not put our dependence in man. "Cease ye from man, whose breath is in his nostrils: for wherein is he to be accounted of?" You must hang your helpless souls upon Jesus. It does not become us to drink from the fountain of the valley, when there is a fountain in the mountain. Let us leave the lower streams; let us come to the higher springs. If there is a point of truth that you do not understand, upon which you do not agree, investigate, compare scripture with scripture, sink the shaft of truth down deep into the mine of God's word. You must lay yourselves and your opinions on the altar of God, put away your preconceived ideas, and let the Spirit of Heaven guide you into all truth.

My brother said at one time that he would not hear anything concerning the doctrine we hold, for fear he should be convinced. He would not come to the meetings, or listen to the discourses; but he afterward declared that he saw he was as guilty as if he had heard them. God had given him an opportunity to know the truth, and he would hold him responsible for this opportunity. There are many among us who are prejudiced against the doctrines that are now being discussed. They will not come to hear, they will not calmly investigate, but they put forth their objections in the dark. They are perfectly satisfied with their position. "Thou sayest, I am rich, and increased with goods, and have need of nothing; and knowest not that thou art wretched, and miserable, and poor, and blind, and naked: I counsel thee to buy of me gold tried in the fire, that thou mayest be rich, and white raiment, that thou mayest be clothed, and that the shame of thy nakedness do not appear; and anoint thine eyes with eye-salve, that thou mayest see. As many as I love, I rebuke and chasten: be zealous therefore, and repent."

This scripture applies to those who live under the sound of the message, but who will not come to hear it. How do you know but that the Lord is giving fresh evidences of his truth, placing it in a new setting, that the way of the Lord may be prepared? What plans have you been laying that new light may be infused through the ranks of God's people? What evidence have you that God has not sent light to his children? All self-sufficiency, egotism, and pride of opinion must be put away. We must come to the feet of Jesus, and learn of him who is meek and lowly of heart. Jesus did not teach his disciples as the rabbis taught theirs. Many of the Jews came and listened as Christ revealed the mysteries of salvation, but they came not to learn; they came to criticise, to catch him in some inconsistency, that they might have something with which to prejudice the people. They were content with their knowledge, but the children of God must know the voice of the true Shepherd. Is not this a time when it would be highly proper to fast and pray before God? We are in danger of variance, in danger of taking sides on a controverted point; and should we not seek God in earnestness, with humiliation of soul, that we may know what is truth?

Nathanael heard John as he pointed to the Saviour, and said, "Behold the Lamb of God, which taketh away the sin of the world!" Nathanael looked at Jesus, but he was disappointed in the appearance of the world's Redeemer. Could he who bore the marks of toil and poverty, be the Messiah? Jesus was a worker; he had toiled with humble working-men, and Nathanael went away. But he did not form his opinion decidedly as to what the character of Jesus was. He knelt down under a fig-tree, inquiring of God if indeed this man was the Messiah. While he was there, Philip came and said, "We have found him, of whom Moses in the law, and the prophets did write, Jesus of Nazareth, the son of Joseph." But the word "Nazareth" again aroused his unbelief, and he said, "Can there any good thing come out of Nazareth?" He was full of prejudice, but Philip did not seek to combat his prejudice; he simply said, "Come and see." When Nathanael came into the presence of Jesus, Jesus said, "Behold an Israelite indeed, in whom is no guile!" Nathanael was amazed. He said, "Whence knowest thou me? Jesus answered and said unto him, Before that Philip called thee, when thou wast under the fig-tree, I saw thee."

Would it not be well for us to go under the fig-tree to plead with God as to what is truth? Would not the eye of God be upon us as it was upon Nathanael? Nathanael believed on the Lord, and exclaimed, "Rabbi, thou art the Son of God; thou art the King of Israel. Jesus answered and said unto him, Because I said unto thee, I saw thee under the fig-tree, believest thou? thou shalt see greater things than these. And he saith unto him, Verily, verily, I say unto you, Hereafter ye shall see heaven open, and the angels of God ascending and descending upon the Son of man."

This is what we shall see if we are connected with God. God wants us to depend upon him, and not upon man. He desires us to have a new heart; he would give us revealings of light from the throne of God. We should wrestle with every difficulty, but when some controverted point is presented, are you to go to man to find out his opinion, and then shape your conclusions from his?–No, go to God. Tell him what you want; take your Bible and search as for hidden treasures.

We do not go deep enough in our search for truth. Every soul who believes present truth will be brought where he will be required to give a reason of the hope that is in him. The people of God will be called upon to stand before kings, princes, rulers, and great men of the earth, and they must know that they do know what is truth. They must be converted men and women. God can teach you more in one moment by his Holy Spirit than you could learn from the great men of the earth. The universe is looking upon the controversy that is going on upon the earth. At an infinite cost, God has provided for every man an opportunity to know that which will make him wise unto salvation. How eagerly do angels look to see who will avail himself of this opportunity! When a message is presented to God's people, they should not rise up in opposition to it; they should go to the Bible, comparing it with the law and the testimony, and if it does not bear this test, it is not true. God wants our minds to expand. He desires to put his grace upon us. We may have a feast of good things every day; for God can open the whole treasure of heaven to us. We are to be one with Christ as he is one with the Father, and the Father will love us as he loves his Son. We may have the same help that Christ had, we may have strength for every emergency; for God will be our front guard and our rereward. He will shut us in on every side, and when we are brought before rulers, before the authorities of the earth, we need not meditate beforehand of what we shall say. God will teach us in the day of our need. Now may God help us to come to the feet of Jesus and learn of him, before we seek to become teachers of others." RH Feb 18, 1890

The Importance of Health Reform In the Preparation of God's People For the Coming of The Lord: E.G.White

"December 10, 1871, I was again shown that the health reform is one branch of the great work which is to fit a people for the coming of the Lord. It is as closely connected with the third angel's message as the hand is with the body. The law of Ten Commandments has been lightly regarded by man, but the Lord would not come to punish the transgressors of that law without first sending them a message of warning. The third angel proclaims that message. Had men ever been obedient to the law of Ten Commandments, carrying out in their lives the principles of those precepts, the curse of disease now flooding the world would not be.

Men and women cannot violate natural law by indulging depraved appetite and lustful passions, and not violate the law of God. Therefore He has permitted the light of health reform to shine upon us, that we may see our sin in violating the laws which He has established in our being. All our enjoyment or suffering may be traced to obedience or transgression of natural law. Our gracious heavenly Father sees the deplorable condition of men who, some knowingly but many ignorantly, are living in violation of the laws that He has established. And in love and pity to the race, He causes the light to shine upon health reform. He publishes His law and the penalty that will follow the transgression of it, that all may learn and be careful to live in harmony with natural law. He proclaims His law so distinctly and makes it so prominent that it is like a city set on a hill. All accountable beings can understand it if they will. Idiots will not be responsible. To make plain natural law, and urge the obedience of it, is the work that accompanies the third angel's message to prepare a people for the coming of the Lord." 3T 161

Appendix B

Theme Songs & Publication List

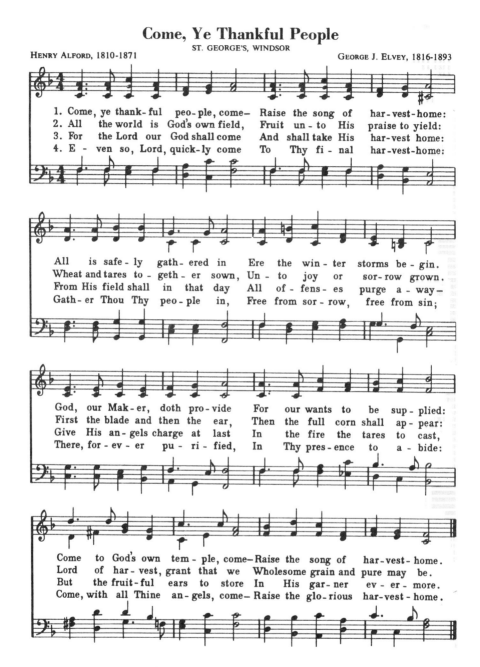

Come, Ye Thankful People
ST. GEORGE'S, WINDSOR

HENRY ALFORD, 1810-1871

GEORGE J. ELVEY, 1816-1893

1. Come, ye thank-ful peo-ple, come— Raise the song of har-vest-home:
2. All the world is God's own field, Fruit un-to His praise to yield:
3. For the Lord our God shall come And shall take His har-vest home:
4. E-ven so, Lord, quick-ly come To Thy fi-nal har-vest-home:

All is safe-ly gath-ered in Ere the win-ter storms be-gin.
Wheat and tares to-geth-er sown, Un-to joy or sor-row grown.
From His field shall in that day All of-fens-es purge a-way—
Gath-er Thou Thy peo-ple in, Free from sor-row, free from sin;

God, our Mak-er, doth pro-vide For our wants to be sup-plied:
First the blade and then the ear, Then the full corn shall ap-pear:
Give His an-gels charge at last In the fire the tares to cast,
There, for-ev-er pu-ri-fied, In Thy pres-ence to a-bide:

Come to God's own tem-ple, come—Raise the song of har-vest-home.
Lord of har-vest, grant that we Wholesome grain and pure may be.
But the fruit-ful ears to store In His gar-ner ev-er-more.
Come, with all Thine an-gels, come— Raise the glo-rious har-vest-home.

Jesus Is Coming Soon

R. E. Winsett

Revive Us Again

WILLIAM P. MACKAY, 1839-1885

JOHN J. HUSBAND, 1760-1825

1. We praise Thee, O God, for the Son of Thy love, For Je - sus who
2. We praise Thee, O God, for Thy Spir- it of light, Who has shown us our
3. All glo - ry and praise to the Lamb that was slain, Who has borne all our
4. Re - vive us a - gain—fill each heart with Thy love; May each soul be re -

died and is now gone a - bove.
Sav - ior and scat - tered our night.   Hal-le - lu-jah, Thine the glo-ry! Hal-le -
sins and has cleansed ev-'ry stain.
kin - dled with fire from a - bove.

CHORUS

lu-jah, a - men! Hal-le - lu-jah, Thine the glo - ry! Re-vive us a - gain.

Publications Available from Truth for the Final Generation

The Powerful Message of the Two Covenants in the Doctrine of Righteousness by Faith

This book seeks to show the difference between the Old and New Covenants, but more importantly to show how loving, compassionate, merciful, and sweet is our gracious God who is not only able but eager to fulfill His promises in our lives.

Elect According to the Foreknowledge of God

Election, predestination and free choice are subjects that have agitated the minds of God's people down through the centuries of the Christian era. If God has foreknown all things are we really free to choose? Is there a true doctrine of predestination? Christians want to make their calling and election sure. Who are the elect? This book seeks to give the Biblical answers to these questions.

The Sealing Work in the Final Generation

The sealing work begins at conversion when the believer's name is entered into the Book of Life. For the final generation, the sealing ends with the believer's name being retained in the Book of Life, after he has passed the great final test and has demonstrated that his mind is fully fixed in loyalty to God.

God's Character—The Best News in the Universe

A study of the character of God from the Bible alone, allowing scripture to interpret scripture. It is dedicated to the ongoing search for truth and the shining light that results from such scriptural research.

The Power of God's Word in the Science of Faith

Many Christians drift along in a superficial experience without appreciating the power of God's word. In this series of studies we discover the victorious power in God's word, and learn to receive and employ that power in the work of overcoming sin.

The New World Economic Order—How Will it Affect You?

The coming new world economic order will usher in sweeping changes to our accustomed way of life, especially the liberties we have enjoyed over the past two hundred years. Necessary reading for the new century.

Notes